A *Historian'*

Other books by David Cecelski

Along Freedom Road

*Democracy Betrayed: The Wilmington Race Riot of 1898
and Its Legacy* (edited with Tim Tyson)

Recollections of My Slavery Days (edited with Kat Charron)

John F. Blair, Publisher
WINSTON-SALEM, NORTH CAROLINA

A *Historian's* Coast

Adventures into the Tidewater Past

by DAVID CECELSKI

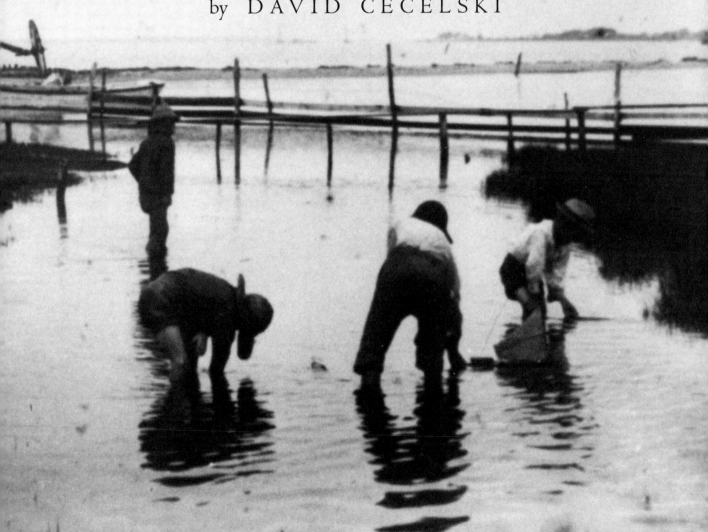

*The paper in this book meets the guidelines for permanence and
durability of the Committee on Production Guidelines for
Book Longevity of the Council on Library Resources.*

Photograph on previous page:
Boys playing with toy boats by a windmill near Beaufort, circa 1900
Courtesy of North Carolina Maritime Museum Collection

Library of Congress Cataloging-in-Publication Data

Cecelski, David S.
A historian's coast : adventures into the Tidewater past / by David Cecelski.
p.   cm.
Includes index.
ISBN 0-89587-189-0 (alk. paper)
1. Atlantic Coast (N.C.)—Description and travel. 2. Atlantic Coast (N.C.)—History.
3. Atlantic Coast (N.C.)—History—Sources. 4. North Carolina—Description and
travel. 5. North Carolina—History. 6. North Carolina—History—Sources. I. Title.

F262.A84 C43 2000
975.6'1dc21
00-029743

Design by Debra Long Hampton

FOUR OYSTER SKIFFS ON SHORE
North Carolina Maritime Museum Collection

*To my mother,
who taught me
to love books.
And to my father,
who taught me
to love boats.*

CONTENTS

WINDMILL AT HATTERAS, SKETCHED BY A UNION SOLDIER DURING THE CIVIL WAR, FROM CHARLES F.
JOHNSON, *THE LONG ROLL*
North Carolina Collection, University of North Carolina Library at Chapel Hill

PREFACE

One winter, when I was a student in Beaufort, North Carolina, I woke every morning before sunrise and piloted a jonboat out to Shackleford Banks. Shackleford is an uninhabited barrier island just south of the Outer Banks. I was researching the ecology of sea grass beds. I never understood why the old salts who ran the boathouse at the Duke University Marine Laboratory allowed a twenty-year-old to take one of their boats on that twelve-mile journey, especially during a winter rife with heavy squalls and nor'easters. All of the other undergraduates worked within a stone's throw of the marine laboratory. I had grown up only a few miles away, and perhaps they believed that I knew the local tides, winds, and shoals better than I really did. All the same, I will never forget those solitary dawns when I guided my boat through the waves, felt the cold salt spray, and watched the sun rise in front of me.

As spring arrived and my mornings at Shackleford Banks grew warmer, I found myself drawn beyond sea grass ecology into other adventures. My first distraction was to lay a crab pot in Back Sound, which I emptied and rebaited every morning on my way back from Shackleford. Then I added a second crab pot, and a third. My blue crabs soon found their way to steaming vats in the kitchen of the marine lab.

One thing led to another. Soon, I staked out a small pound net to catch fish in a little bay at Shackleford. Sometimes, I raked clams. Other times, I harvested scallops and oysters. When I discovered that the head chef at the marine lab, a retired navy cook named Tommy Morton, was allergic to all seafood except conchs, I began to pick up a few at Bird Shoal. Tommy turned the conchs into tantalizing fritters and stews. Eventually, the boathouse crew, housekeepers, and scientists alike were placing special orders with me, and I rambled far and wide not to disappoint them.

Fishing was not my only distraction that spring. I also began to linger with the local watermen I met while I was working on the sea grass beds. An old clammer from Mill Creek got into the habit of taking his coffee break on my shoal. I learned a down-to-earth, personal history of the early twentieth century from his stories that I never forgot during my graduate studies at Harvard. At the fish camps on Shackleford Banks, old-time Downeasterners showed me the graveyards where their ancestors were buried before the great hurricane of 1899 washed away the last of the local communities. And on my way back down Taylor Creek, I often tarried at the wharf by Piggy Potter's fish factory. There, old fishermen with biceps like ham hocks told me of the waning schools of menhaden that they had to chase all the way to Florida.

Before long, I realized that I was as excited to hear those stories of the past as I was intrigued by the ecology of the sea. The stories seemed to get right at the marrow of our humanity. They revealed a human history entwined with ecological upheaval, and they exposed an intimacy between the coastal landscape and people that seemed profound enough to encompass my scientific interests. I never lost my intellectual enthusiasm for marine biology, yet it eventually led me to become not a scientist who studies the sea, but a historian who writes about the sea's edge.

The essays in *A Historian's Coast*, originally

published in *Coastwatch* magazine, are a lot like my meandering adventures on the way to and from Shackleford Banks: they are not exactly what I was supposed to be doing. I was researching and writing a scholarly book on slavery and freedom in the maritime society of the antebellum South. I was also directing a long-term oral history research project about the World War II home front on the North Carolina coast, a study based at the Southern Oral History Program at the University of North Carolina at Chapel Hill. But along the way, I discovered such precious treasures as a rare eighteenth-century travel journal, a never-before-heard oral history, the yellowed parchment of a sea traveler's diary, and a slave's firsthand reminiscences. I wanted to explore the unknown worlds of their pasts and glean whatever insights might lie within them. I came to relish my historical side trips along the North Carolina coastline as much as the daily devotions of my regular scholarship.

The essays in *A Historian's Coast* are about the tangled ties that bind humans to the coast and tidewater of North Carolina. Most are grounded in one rare or little-known historical source— sometimes one that I discovered. Whenever possible, I explored the places described in them by foot or in one of my boats to learn how the landscape has changed over the generations. All of these essays are adventures into the past, but perhaps they will also be useful in our current struggle to cherish and preserve both our coastal waters and the stories that have grown up beside them. I hope you relish them with the same spirit that I did Tommy Morton's conch chowder, and in as good company as I found along the water's edge when I was supposed to be working.

A Note to Readers

NET SPREADS ON TAYLOR CREEK, BEAUFORT, NORTH CAROLINA, CIRCA 1880
North Carolina Maritime Museum Collection

The essays in *A Historian's Coast* appeared originally in *Coastwatch* magazine, which is published six times a year by the North Carolina Sea Grant College Program. I have made minor revisions in them all for this book.

I have also included a dozen excerpts from some of the most interesting historical sources on which the essays are based. In those cases, I have adhered to the spelling, grammar, and punctuation used in the original documents except in a few cases, where I have noted the exception in the text.

DR. DAVID PHELPS
Photograph by Michael Halminski

THE SMOKE
AND ASHES OF CROATAN

At least a thousand years before the English landed at Roanoke Island, the Algonquians lived along our tidewater and Outer Banks. Their relics are everywhere. I find their pottery shards in freshly plowed corn and cotton fields. I stumble upon their arrowheads by the edges of creeks and bays. I see their architectural handiwork in the Crossing Path at Mill Creek, Shell Point at Harkers Island, the Old Indian Canal at Turnagain Bay.

These last traces of the Algonquian past are in danger of being destroyed by coastal development. The builders of strip malls, highways, and golf courses have granted them no asylum. Moving too fast to realize what they are doing, developers pave over Indian burial sites and scatter the remains of ancient villages. Fortunately, new archaeological research, much of it led by Dr. David Phelps at East Carolina University, offers a crucial chance to deepen our understanding of coastal Native Americans before bulldozers literally scatter the last of their bones.

Recently, I joined Phelps at one of the most important archaeological digs: the legendary village of Croatan. In 1993, Hurricane Emily's twelve-foot tidal swell exposed a section of an Algonquian village in a dune ridge at Buxton on Hatteras Island. That dune ridge had been identified by archaeologist William Haag in 1956 and again by Phelps in 1983 as the likely site of the Croatan chiefdom's capital. So far, eight archaeological sites have been discovered at

Hatteras Island, including an ossuary—a mass burial—of the Algonquian nobility.

First charted on a map by English surveyor John White in 1586, the Croatan chiefdom stretched from present-day Buxton south to Ocracoke Inlet. The capital village, also known as Croatan, was located by an old inlet called Chacandepeco that cut through the island immediately north of Cape Hatteras. It was one of the few places on the Outer Banks with a maritime forest extensive enough to safeguard an archaeological site from the region's winds and storms.

The shelter of Buxton Woods also explains why Croatan was the only Algonquian chiefdom with a capital village on the Outer Banks when the English arrived. The Croatans had good soil for their cornfields, orchards, and gardens; ample forest for fuel and hunting; and certainly no shortage of fish and shellfish. Phelps estimates that as many as five thousand people lived in the chiefdom.

The Croatans played a key role in English–Native American diplomacy during the Roanoke Island voyages between 1584 and 1587. Most famously, Croatan may have been the destination of the Lost Colony, the first effort by the English to colonize North America. When the colonists disappeared from Roanoke Island in 1587, they left only one clue of their whereabouts: a gatepost carved with the word *Croatoan.*

The fate of the Lost Colony has been argued heatedly for years. It is no wonder that when Phelps, using geological records and sixteenth-century maps, concluded that the Buxton site was almost certainly Croatan, scholars and journalists worldwide began to speculate about whether the Lost Colony had finally been found.

Even though I had never participated in an archaeological dig, Phelps, his East Carolina University assistants, and a devoted group of Buxton volunteers welcomed me with warm hospitality. Then they handed me a shovel and put me to work. For two days, I dug in a live oak glade along a sandy ridge by Pamlico Sound. I sliced through wax myrtle and poison ivy roots with a razor-sharp shovel, then dug several feet deeper into the sand. Working on my hands and knees, I gently removed layers of soil an inch or two at a time with a tiny trowel, as the archaeologists taught me. Then we sifted the soil for fragments of the past.

The earth had not forgotten the Algonquians. Deep under matted roots and barren sand, Croatan was imprinted into a layer of dark, shell-laden midden eighteen inches thick. We found copper beads and pipe stems, stone flakes and tools, shell piles and deer bones (ancient garbage), and shards of Colington period (800–1650 A.D.) pottery that was coiled, pressed, and tempered with oyster shells. Dark shadows revealed where posts once supported village buildings.

We also unearthed European relics: lead shot, gun flints, nails, Delphic pottery. Radiocarbon dating indicated that these artifacts, like the Algonquian remains, originated in the early colonial period, between 1650 and 1715, several generations after the Lost Colony. They were probably used as trading items between the English and Croatans.

Several days after I left Buxton, the East Carolina investigators found English farthings (copper coins) dating from the 1670s. Holes were drilled through them, a sign that the Croatans used the coins for decoration, not money. They were found along with bird-bone rings and strong evidence that the Croatans were manufacturing lead buckshot. Phelps's team discovered iron tools for molding the shot and hundreds of tiny, hardened puddles of lead.

Phelps will be pleasantly surprised—maybe stunned—if his team actually finds evidence of the Lost Colony. Like most historians, he believes the forsaken colonists traveled to southern Chesapeake Bay. There, they most likely met an untimely demise at the hands of the Powhatans, the powerful confederacy headed by Pocahontas's father. This was the story told by the Jamestown colony's secretary, William Strachey, writing in his *Historie of Travell into Virginia Britania* in 1612.

The colonists may have gone to Croatan briefly, however. Manteo, one of two Native Americans who visited London with Sir Arthur Barlowe in 1584, was a Croatan, and his mother was head of the Croatan chiefdom. Manteo aligned with the English when other villages—Aquascogoc, Dasemunkepeuc, and Secotan—joined forces against the Roanoke colonists in 1587. Having treated the Native Americans harshly during their brief sojourn at Roanoke Island, the English had very few native allies. It would not be surprising if they looked to Croatan for temporary sanctuary.

Even if Phelps does not solve the mystery of the Lost Colony, the Croatan dig promises to cast piercing new light on other mysteries about the coastal Algonquians and their seventeenth-century encounters with the English.

The British had little presence in North Carolina for sixty years after the Roanoke Island colonists disappeared. After 1650, however, the English pushed the colonial frontier south from Virginia. Conflicts quickly arose between natives and newcomers over hunting, fishing, grazing, and land rights.

Early on, the Algonquians and their Iroquoian neighbors successfully resisted English intrusions. On the eve of the eighteenth century, they still outnumbered the European colonists. But they soon succumbed to pandemics of smallpox, influenza, and other Old World diseases. The Algonquian chiefdoms were all destroyed or subjugated by English forces by the end of the Tuscarora War of 1711–13.

Only the broadest outline of these Native Americans' final reign can be detected in historical documents, and we know nothing from their point of view. The coastal natives were annihilated in six and a half decades, between 1650 and 1715, and archaeological digs such as the one at Croatan are the only way that we will ever learn more about them.

The Croatan capital disappeared, too. In its heyday, the village stretched at least half a mile along Pamlico Sound and Chacandepeco Inlet. But when English surveyor John Lawson published his *New Voyage to Carolina* in 1709, he reported only "16 fighting men" at Croatan (by then known as Hatteras). In 1733, Edward Mosely made the last known reference to natives at the site. On a North Carolina map published in London, he scribbled, "Indians, none now inhabiting the See Coast, but about 6 or 8 at Hatteras."

During my visit to Buxton, I talked late into the nights with the East Carolina archaeologists.

On those warm summer evenings, Phelps unfurled vivid imaginary maps of the Croatan capital. Listening to him, I envisioned the bustling village. I pictured long houses, covered with grass mats, scattered along the inlet, broad cornfields tangled with squash and bean vines, elegant fishing weirs in Pamlico Sound, and Croatan boatmen crisscrossing the sound to trade with English and native villages.

We also talked about history and archaeology, the smoke and ashes of our past. At the Buxton dig, I was struck by how patiently the archaeologists worked. They toiled with painstaking rigor, an inch at a time. They seemed burdened by the knowledge that they, unlike historians, had but one chance to retrieve the past. To an archaeologist, the earth confides its mysteries only once. After the East Carolina team has dug, sifted, sorted, classified, and refilled the Croatan site, it can never be studied again. The work cannot be hurried and must be done right the first time.

It is a duty I do not envy. For now, as new condominiums and beach resorts lay claim to coastal lands, there is no time for patience.

EXCAVATING SHELL MIDDEN AT THE SITE
OF CROATAN ON HATTERAS ISLAND
Photograph by Michael Halminski

SORTING THE MIDDEN FOR
ALGONQUIAN RELICS
Photograph by Michael Halminski

THE SHORES OF LAKE ELLIS (CRAVEN COUNTY), CIRCA. 1925
G. A. Nicholl Photograph Album, New Bern-Craven County Public Library

A HISTORIAN'S COAST

THE LAMB'S ARMY

In 1753, an English missionary named Catharine Phillips passed through some of the most remote swamps and forests along the North Carolina coast. She was only twenty-seven years old, three thousand miles from home, and among strangers.

Six years earlier, she had received the call to preach at a Quaker meeting in her native Dudley, in Worcestershire. "Having now entered the list of publick combatants in the Lamb's army," she wrote, "I pretty soon became concerned to travel for the promotion of truth and righteousness."

Published in London in 1797, *Memories of the Life of Catharine Phillips* is one of the rarest of the many journals, diaries, and memoirs penned by missionaries who evangelized in the Carolina tide-water during the late seventeenth and early eighteenth centuries. Quaker missionary William Edmundson, who proselytized along the coast in 1671, may have been the first such writer. In his journal, he described remote forests that were "all wilderness [with] no English inhabitants or pathways" and that had only "marked trees to guide people."

Fuming at earthly pleasures in the colony's bedraggled, rum-soaked little ports and backcountry villages, few of those early ministers and lay preachers could boast much success in the soul-saving way. The colony eventually attracted a variety of religious outcasts and dissenters—Quakers, Baptists, and Moravians among them—but overall, few tidewater people joined churches or looked for evangelical preaching in colonial days.

But if they rarely drew large crowds to their makeshift altars, these itinerant preachers still left priceless troves of documents chronicling the colonial landscape, a world of vast longleaf pine forests, uncharted pocosins, and great cypress and juniper swamps. The missionaries' accounts, like Phillips's *Memories*, also reveal much about the colonists' spiritual outlook toward what to them was a strange, new land.

Catharine Phillips was unusual among the exhorters and evangelists. It was, after all, a day when women did not travel by themselves and were rarely allowed to preach in public; often, they were excluded even from praying aloud in their own churches. At one point, while visiting a Friends meeting along the Perquimans River, Phillips humbly acknowledged that the novelty of an itinerant woman preacher might explain her drawing power. "No women-ministers had visited part of this country before us," she wrote, "so that the people were probably excited by curiosity."

Yet a woman missionary like Phillips may not have been an altogether rare sight, at least not in 1753. The Quakers had always held that God's "inner light" could be found equally in every person, and they did not discourage women from becoming "public preachers," as the Religious Society of Friends called its missionaries. Phillips came from a Quaker family. Her father, a paralytic by the time she left home in 1748, had been a Quaker missionary. In North Carolina, she found a sizable Quaker community that was at least respectful toward her.

The Quakers were not the only sect in which large numbers of women become religious leaders during the First Great Awakening, as the religious revivals that swept the colonies in the 1730s and 1740s are collectively known. Women also played leadership roles in the New Light, Separate, and Baptist faiths—all evangelical, dissenting churches. The pattern was repeated by the Freewill Baptists, the Methodists, and other evangelical faiths during the Second Great Awakening a half-century later.

The hardships of travel were a constant lament in colonial writings by missionaries, man or woman. As early as 1672, the great Quaker missionary George Fox described the North Carolina coastal plains as being "pretty full of great bogs and swamps; so that we were commonly wet to the knees, and lay abroad a-nights in the woods by a fire."

Until the Tuscarora War of 1711–13, English missionaries often felt threatened by the native Algonquian, Siouan, and Iroquoian peoples as well. On his second visit to North Carolina, in 1676,

George Edmundson preached in the vicinity of the Great Dismal Swamp, where he found "perillous travelling [,] for the Indians were not subdued. . . . Scarce any durst travel that way unarmed." His use of the word *wilderness* to describe lands where native peoples had villages gives insight into the way many missionaries saw coastal Indians. The natives, too, were part of a wilderness in need of "civilization."

Travel had not improved much for missionaries by the time Catharine Phillips arrived in America. After disembarking in Charleston, South Carolina, in late October 1753, Phillips and a companion, Mary Peisley, followed the Pee Dee River toward a Quaker settlement at Haw River, in Alamance County, North Carolina. After riding all day through a dark, lonely forest, the women and their guides made camp by a swamp. They slept under "a little shed of the branches of pine-trees, on a rising sandy ground, which abounded with lofty pines."

Many English missionaries found the colonial backcountry strange and threatening. Villages were a rare sight, and travel through the dense forests and ubiquitous swamps was slow. Something about the great forests cast long shadows in colonial travelers' minds. They looked with revulsion at this remote realm and the pitch makers, trappers, and dirt farmers who lived there. "You don't know gloominess until you travel through that country," a woman named Mary Harper Beall wrote years later, making almost a moral judgment against the colony's great stretches of woods and wetlands.

The indictment was harsher yet among high-minded preachers, who looked at tidewater wild places as a dangerous sanctuary for fugitive slaves and for Indians who had outlasted the Tuscarora War. At times, they preached as if clearing forests and draining swamps were a holy crusade blessed by God, as much a part of colonizing America as thwarting the French and the Indians.

They likewise associated the deep forests and coastal swamps with a whole host of European outcasts who had taken refuge in the colony: criminals, debtors, women who had fled their marriages, indentured servants who had escaped bondage in other colonies. In 1711, a frustrated Anglican minister, John Urmston, lambasted the Carolina colonists as former convicts from English prisons, then called them "the most notorious profligates upon earth." Many itinerant ministers, especially Anglicans, seemed to find the colony's untamed landscape somehow symbolic of those dissenters and pariahs. They compared the countryside unfavorably with England, where game wardens maintained the forests as hunting parks and poachers risked the death penalty.

Armed with that moral righteousness, many

colonial evangelists saw the devil's stomping grounds in the longleaf pine glades and blackwater swamps. From their pulpits, they exhorted against the dark, unruly forces of the wilderness. They taught children to treat the woods as an asylum for evil spirits and witches.

The Reverend Ruben Ross long recalled how he had learned to fear the forest dwellers near his home in Williamston. "We village people could tell a witch as far as we could see one, as we thought," he told his son and biographer. "When they came to town, they always appeared in the form of little old women, with bright scarlet cloaks and hoods drawn over the head."

Catharine Phillips shared little of the moral-tinged fear of the wilderness so prevalent among her evangelical brethren. She seemed a peaceful soul even that first night camping by a swamp: "We made a large fire, and it being a calm, fair, moon-light night, we spent it cheerfully, though we slept but little."

Not that the coastal wilderness never tested her faith. Phillips often slept in cold, damp lodgings, if not outdoors. One winter day, she fell backward into the water while crossing a swamp on the way to a Quaker meeting in Bladen County. She was frightened by stories that a panther had recently killed a traveler in what was probably the Green Swamp, about forty miles west of Wilmington. She was also startled by the barking of wolves near her camp. For another half-century, both of those predators still roamed the Green Swamp.

Phillips traveled to Alamance County, visiting Quaker meetings at New Garden, Eno River, and other places, then rode all the way back to Bladen County and Wilmington. Then, on January 20, 1754, she set out for the colony's largest Quaker settlements, which had been founded above Albemarle Sound in the seventeenth century. She traveled north through the ports of New Bern and Washington. "In this journey we met with considerable hardships," she remembered, "the people amongst whom we were being very poor, their houses cold, and provisions mean."

Arriving at the Perquimans River on February 6, she preached at the Piney Woods meeting in Perquimans County and the Old Neck meeting in Pasquotank County. She also held prayer services, mainly for non-Quakers, in the villages of Edenton and Bath. Though the counties north of Albemarle Sound were at that time the most densely settled in North Carolina, they still had few churches or ministers. In Bath, as in so many places she visited, Phillips found that "the life of religion was scarcely so much as known by many of [the residents]."

Bath, the colony's oldest town, was the scene of the two most unforgettable incidents in *Memories of the Life of Catharine Phillips*.

The first was the death of Rebecca Tombs, a "valuable friend" whom Phillips met at a Quaker meeting near the Perquimans River. Tombs volunteered to accompany Phillips to Bath. They crossed Albemarle Sound on a chilly day when "the frost was so hard, that the water . . . was frozen some distance from the shore." Tombs grew ill in the harsh weather as they rode another

"In Sweet Peace"

We set out for Carver's Creek, a journey of about 160 miles, through an almost uninhabited country. We were accompanied by John Wright and J. Pigot, friends. The accommodation we met with was very mean, but rendered easy, under a sense of our being in the way of our duty. At one place where we lodged, the room wherein we lay was exposed to the weather on almost every side, and it being a wet night, the rain beat in upon us in bed; but my mind was preserved in sweet peace, and under some degree of a sense of Divine favour. The woman of the house was a tender spirit, and appeared to be seeking after substantial good. I had considerable freedom to speak to her on religious subjects; which she took well, and I was thankful that our lots were cast under the same roof.

Another night, we lay in the woods, with tolerable comfort, though the weather was cold, and the ground damp. About two hours before we stopped, as I was attempting to cross a swamp on some loose pieces of wood, one of them rolled, and threw me backward into it. One of our friends was leading me, and the other, seeing me in danger of falling, stepped behind me into the swamp, and caught me, so that I was wet but on one side, except my feet: and, although I mounted my horse immediately after putting on a dry pair of stockings, rode in my wet clothes, and lay down in them, I was preserved from taking cold. In the night two of our horses strayed away from us, and our guides were obliged to leave us and go in quest of them; so that we were several hours ourselves in this wilderness, surrounded,

for aught we knew, by bears, wolves, and panthers. Before we pitched our tent, I had been intimidated by an account which had been given me respecting the panthers infesting that quarter; one of which it was said had killed a person not very far distant from this spot; but when we were thus left, all fear was removed, and we spent the time of our friends' absence cheerfully. I went without the shelter of our shed, and renewed our fire with some wood our friends had gathered. The fire, under Providence, was probably our preservation from those ferocious animals.

It was a fine moon-light night, our friends traced our horses' footsteps in the sand for about three miles in the way we had come, and found them feeding in some luxuriant canes. The sagacious animals probably observed them as they came to the spot where we pitched our tent, and having but poor feeding there, went back to fill their bellies. As we proceeded on our journey, some of our company discovered the track of a wild beast in the sand, which gave room to suspect that they had been near our tents in the night; but we were preserved from their fury, and from being affrighted by their hideous howl. However, as we rode through the woods in the morning, we heard the barking of wolves at a small distance from us, but a rising ground prevented us from seeing them.

From Catharine Phillips,
*Memories of the
Life of Catharine Phillips*
(1797)

forty-three miles along the edge of the East Dismal Swamp to Bath.

After preaching at the Bath courthouse, Tombs was "seized with an ague." Phillips "soon became apprehensive of her being removed by death." They headed back to the Perquimans River and sent a messenger ahead to alert Tombs's husband of her illness, but, in Phillips's words, "the Almighty did not see fit to continue her in pain." Rebecca Tombs died on the morning of February 20, 1754. Phillips had a coffin built and brought the corpse home to the Perquimans River, where a widower and seven motherless children waited.

Phillips did not pretend to be unaffected by the long journey across the East Dismal and Albemarle Sound with her new friend's corpse. Her native England was hardly a stranger to morbid illnesses and short lives, but Phillips never grew used to the high incidence of infectious diseases in colonial America and the often quick, fatal results. Faulting herself for allowing Tombs to accompany her to Bath, she confessed that sometimes, "like Jonah, I wished to die."

The second incident at Bath gives a sense of where the young English evangelist saw the root of evil, if not in longleaf glades or cypress swamps like so many of her countrymen. It was a relatively small affair concerning a slave girl, but it clearly made a lasting impression on Phillips. "One night a poor negro girl fell asleep at the top of the stairs, near our chamber door," she wrote, and the innkeeper, "seeing her there[,] kicked her down them." The innkeeper had "a dark ferocious disposition," she observed. "Indeed, darkness seemed to surround us in this house."

This incident brings to mind an earlier passage in Phillips's *Memories* when she was passing through the Green Swamp. Having failed to reach their destination at a remote inn, she and her party were forced to camp in a swampy tract renowned for its wolves, bear, and panthers. The next day, they breakfasted at the inn, where Phillips encountered "a wicked set of company, who had spent the night there."

Reticent about why she deemed the inn's guests so wicked, Phillips was nonetheless spurred by their behavior to contrast nature and humanity. Here, she turned upside down many preachers' views of the colonial landscape. Considering the inn's guests, she rejoiced that she and her fellow travelers had stayed in the swamp instead of the inn. "It appeared much more comfortable," she wrote, "to be under the open canopy of heaven, and the protection of Providence, though among the wild beasts, than among those of the human race."

WHAT THE
GOVERNOR GREW

Whenever I visit Tryon Palace in New Bern, I head straight to the kitchen garden. As an avid backyard gardener, I cannot wait to see what new heirloom vegetables and long-forgotten herbs grow in this garden, modeled after the kind popular when Governor William Tryon occupied the palace in 1770–71. I am sure many visitors prefer to see how English colonists dressed for high tea, but garden buffs like me want to see how they fertilized their turnips.

As re-created by landscape architect Morley Williams in the 1950s, Tryon Palace's kitchen garden is an expansive, 16,200-square-foot plot surrounded by an 8-foot-high brick wall. Resplendent with vegetables, herbs, and fruit trees, the garden beds are divided into quadrants sepa-

rated by walkways, with two dipping wells in the middle. Adorning the garden walls is a wide array of espaliers, which are fruit trees that have been pruned into formal patterns against a wall or fence.

Judging from his surviving letters, Governor Tryon never paid much notice to the kitchen garden. He had his hands full ruling a colony on the verge of revolution against England. He is best remembered for putting down the Regulators, Piedmont farmers who revolted in 1771. Tryon may have left the garden's care to his cook. Unfortunately, we do not know who prepared the meals for his family in New Bern. Learning that would possibly tell us much about the kitchen garden. Tryon employed a French chef named Pierre LeBlanc when he was governor at

Brunswick, the colonial capital before the palace was built in New Bern in 1769. The next Royal governor, Josiah Martin, had an African American cook whose name we do not know.

Historical records say almost nothing about what grew in Tryon Palace's kitchen garden. Only because of a 1775 incident in which Governor Martin was accused of hiding a barrel of gunpowder "under a fine bed of cabbage" for use against the American revolutionaries do we know with certainty the name of any vegetable grown there. Even the kitchen garden's original design was a mystery until just a few years ago. In 1991, Tryon Palace researchers discovered the garden plan at the Academica Nacional de la Historia in Venezuela. The building's architect, John Hawks, had given it to a Venezuelan traveler named Francisco de Miranda when he passed through New Bern in 1783.

Even without the kind of detailed journals that Thomas Jefferson left of his famed kitchen garden at Monticello, the Tryon Palace gardeners have tried admirably to capture the soul of the original kitchen garden. In addition to scavenging every mention of gardening and cookery from eighteenth-century travel accounts, they have drawn on the classic texts of early American gardening, such as Philip Miller's *Gardener's Dictionary* (1754), and on lists of ingredients in early American cookbooks such as Amelia Simmons's *American Cookery* (1796) and Mary Randolph's *Virginia House-wife* (1828).

They also realize that the original kitchen garden would have contained an extraordinary mix of American, European, and African crops. The colonial gardeners would have combined sweet potatoes, peppers, green beans, and squash cultivated by Native Americans; cabbages, peas, turnips, and other vegetables found in any English garden; and okra, watermelons, and eggplant, whose seeds probably arrived in America aboard slave ships from Africa. All can be found in the kitchen garden today.

Several features distinguish the kitchen garden at Tryon Palace from modern vegetable gardens like mine. Perhaps most importantly, the palace's garden holds many vegetables rarely grown or eaten in the United States today. Since the eighteenth century, for example, new lettuce hybrids have displaced many other leafy greens in American diets. But at Tryon Palace, visitors can still find dandelions, sorrel (which adds a lemony flavor to salads), and creasy greens grown for the dinner table, as well as small shrubs like hyssop (*Hyssopus officinalis*), a pungently aromatic plant used to flavor salads, soups, and meat dishes.

A greater variety of root crops would also have been grown in Tryon Palace's kitchen garden. The

THE KITCHEN GARDEN AT TRYON PALACE
Courtesy of Tryon Palace Historic Sites and Gardens

Irish potato, actually cultivated by ancestors of the Incas at least six thousand years before it was grown in Ireland, later overshadowed other root crops in American gardens, but that was not yet the case in the 1770s. At Tryon Palace, visitors find still-common roots such as radishes, carrots, beets, sweet potatoes, turnips, and onions. Turnips, in fact, were wildly popular vegetables in colonial gardens, far more so than today. The Tryon Palace garden also includes root crops not very common now, such as parsnips, skirrets, and salsify. Stewed, baked, or used in cream sauce, salsify (*Tragopogon porrifolius*) is known as the "oyster plant" because its flavor resembles that of fried oysters.

Cardoon is another vegetable grown at Tryon Palace that has fallen out of favor. Cultivated for at least three thousand years, cardoon (*Cynarra cardunculus*) is an ancestor of the globe artichoke. Colonial cooks blanched its stalks like celery and served them as a side dish, in stews and soups, pickled, and dipped in batter and fried.

Other vegetables grown in my backyard garden may not belong in the kitchen garden at Tryon Palace. The most notable is the tomato. Named from the Aztec word *tomatl*, the tomato was originally a weedy, small-fruited native of Peru, Chile, Bolivia, and Ecuador north to Mexico. Spanish conquistadors found the *tomatl* growing in Emperor Montezuma's gardens in 1519 and carried it to Europe. There, it became an essential part of many cuisines, especially in southern Italy, where it was called the *pomodoro* (golden apple). The tomato was greeted more skeptically in England, however, and it was not described as a food plant in the American colonies until Jefferson's *Garden Book* in 1781. It is uncertain if tomatoes were yet grown in New Bern during Tryon's governorship.

Unlike most backyard gardens today, the kitchen garden also holds a wide variety of heirloom vegetables. Most modern vegetables are fairly recent hybrids. Since only a few corporate agribusinesses monopolize the seed market, relatively few plant varieties are cultivated. A growing number of gardeners purposefully collect and raise old varieties (known as heirlooms) to preserve them. Finding heirloom varieties dating to Tryon's day is difficult but not impossible. One of the carrot varieties at Tryon Palace today—the Long Orange Improved—dates to Dutch breeders in 1620 and has been cultivated in North America for 350 years.

The kitchen garden at Tryon Palace also mingles herbs and vegetables, a practice true to the colonial period but much less common today, as gardeners tend to cultivate separate plots for their herbs. The herbs in the original kitchen garden were used for both culinary and medicinal

SCARLETT RUNNER BEAN, *PHASEOLUS COCCINEUS*
Courtesy of Tryon Palace Historic Sites and Gardens

purposes. Julie Craig, the current kitchen gardener, grows dozens of herb varieties, including hyssop, which was used as a purgative and emetic; mints, used to soothe external inflammation; lovage, used as a diuretic and for relief of gas; and valerian, used as a tranquilizer and calmative.

Many of the herbs grown in the kitchen garden had uses in colonial days that are unfamiliar to us now. Hops, best known today as a beer ingredient, can be eaten boiled and buttered like asparagus; it was also used to treat insomnia and liver problems and as a source of yellow dye for wool. Soapwort (*Saponaria officinalis*) made an excellent skin cleanser and shampoo. Lavender, of course, produces a sweet fragrance; it was also used to treat stress-related headaches and to prevent moth damage in woolens.

One of the most interesting projects at the Tryon Palace kitchen garden is an investigation into colonial fertilizers and pesticides. Organic gardening, often considered something of a fad today, was the universal practice in Governor Tryon's era. Julie Craig fertilizes the kitchen garden with horse manure, compost, and crab meal, much as colonial gardeners did. She avoids the potentially harmful effects of synthetic pesticides by experimenting with different pesticides used in the colonial period, including soap, tobacco dust, tea, and smoke blown over the plants.

In the nineteenth century, the kind of walled English garden re-created in New Bern fell out of fashion. But as kitchen gardens spread into backyards and fields, coastal residents discovered the pleasures of seeing out in the open their flowering vines, brightly colored tomatoes and pumpkins, and the sculpturelike elegance of stakes and trellises. Today, vegetable gardens remain a source of pride and joy for many of us, and one of the best reminders that beauty and practicality can go hand in hand.

HENRY ANSELL'S RECOLLECTIONS OF KNOTTS ISLAND

A nor'easter was blowing an icy mist across Currituck Sound when I visited Knotts Island. I walked along Great Marsh for hours and never saw another soul. Even the tundra swans and snow geese had retreated into thickets; I heard only a solitary marsh rail beckoning somewhere far off. A real tempest was blowing, but I hardly noticed: I had come to this remote peninsula between the North Landing River and Currituck Sound, just south of Virginia, to mark the anniversary of a far worse storm that hit Knotts Island many, many years ago.

On March 6, 1846—exactly 150 years before my visit—the most wicked nor'easter of modern times hit Knotts Island. Descending from the North Atlantic in bone-chilling fury, the storm drove snowy gray breakers across Currituck Banks and into Knotts Island. Fish camps and gunners'

homes disappeared under the waves. Dunes and forests vanished overnight. Mariners caught at sea could only be pitied and, later, mourned.

A storm like that bears remembering. And in truth, I had wanted to visit Knotts Island since I first read about the nor'easter of 1846 in Henry Beasley Ansell's "Recollections of a Life Time and More." Born on Knotts Island in 1832, Ansell spent most of his life there and in Coinjock, on the mainland of Currituck County. Sometime around 1907, after he had retired as county surveyor and clerk of court, he began to write the story of his boyhood years. Never published, his handwritten recollections are now preserved in the Southern Historical Collection of the University of North Carolina at Chapel Hill.

Before the hurricane of 1828 closed New Currituck Inlet, Knotts Island was a busy maritime community linked by the inlet to foreign ports and their ways. "Sailors from North and South met here," Ansell recalled his elders telling him. Cut off from the sea, Knotts Island languished as Currituck Sound went from salt water to fresh water. The salt marshes died; the great oyster beds vanished; the mullet and flounder disappeared. Without a navigable inlet, Knotts Island was suddenly a lonely backwater.

During Ansell's boyhood, a new economy haltingly unfolded at Knotts Island. Thick growths of freshwater grasses gradually blanketed Currituck Sound. The tender grasses attracted huge flocks of migratory ducks and geese, and waterfowl gunning, not maritime trade or commercial fishing, became the island's major industry. Led by local gunners Wilson Cooper and Timothy Bowden, the Knotts Islanders pioneered new ways of waterfowl hunting, including the use of better muskets and wooden decoys. They shipped their prizes by the thousands to far-off cities. And even if islanders no longer had oysters to harvest, they could send freshwater fish such as perch and chub to Norfolk's markets.

Then, in early March 1846, a stiff breeze blew from the northeast, increasing bit by bit every day for a week. "The wind still increased," Ansell remembered. "The old Atlantic was plunging on its shore with a mighty roar, as if a squadron of modern war ships were practicing their heavy artillery." When the storm finally reached its full strength, "the creaking joints of the housetops and the roaring of the blast in the tall old trees, mingled with the ocean's roar, were appalling." Old-timers had not seen a storm like it since the American Revolution. Ansell never forgot how, in his words, "all stood aghast."

For two nights and a day, the winds blew with increasing rage. Then, without abating at all, they shifted a bit north, and snow began to fall. "The next morning found devastation complete—trees uprooted and in confusion; the earth strewn with limbs and boughs, and covered with three inches of snow," Ansell recalled.

The Knotts Islanders at last ventured warily into the dying gale. Ansell and his father walked down to the marshy freshwater bay between Knotts Island and Currituck Banks. "Such a sight," Ansell wrote, "was never seen before." Rising on a spring tide, the storm had buried Currituck Banks. "No marsh, no beach, nothing [was] to be seen oceanward except a few tops of the large mounting sandhills." A stunned Ansell found that "the great salt waves were breaking at our feet."

Knotts Island had been devastated. The nor'easter had washed away homes and fences. Graveyards were upturned. Great schools of chub perished when the ocean's waves rolled over the

WRECK OF THE STEAMSHIP *METROPOLIS* AT CURRITUCK BEACH FROM *FRANK LESLIE'S ILLUSTRATED NEWSPAPER*, DECEMBER 2, 1878. SCENES LIKE THIS WERE COMMON ON THE OUTER BANKS.
North Carolina Collection, University of North Carolina Library, Chapel Hill

Henry Ansell's Recollections of Knotts Island

bay. Corpses of hogs, cattle, and sheep bobbed in the surf.

As the islanders gathered by the bay, someone asked what had become of the only two families that lived on Currituck Banks directly across from Knotts Island. Cooper and Bowden, the two expert gunners, were native Knotts Islanders. They had moved to Currituck Banks to be closer to the waterfowl grounds. When the Knotts Islanders learned that the families were missing, they sent out a rescue party. Borrowing Colonel John B. Jones's fishing boat, thirteen volunteers ventured directly into the nor'easter's headwinds to find them. "With sturdy oars, these men rowed against waves and flood and gale over bay and marsh," Ansell wrote.

"The Water Was Very Thickly Stirred by Something"

The people of the Island had not as yet foreseen their main loss, and did not do so for some months thereafter. This Island is bordered on its west side, almost its entire length, by a swamp, or low woodland which was then set densely in good timber of heart pine. When it came time for these trees to commence their summer's growth they died, together with all the fire wood and rail-timber on the adjacent knolls; from this loss the Island to this day has not recovered, not can it ever recover. This timber produced large quantities of lightwood much needed in those days; and, after these storms, it grew scarcer and scarcer as the years rolled on, and at present little can be found.

The following Summer, by some freak of nature, a lone pine here and there could be seen dressed in living green, standing like a solitary sentinel guarding his dead comrades under a flag of truce, waiting for the burial party. Six feet of salt water had stood among these trees, as could be ascertained by the drift lodged on their trunks.

So the injury could now be seen complete;—hogs, cattle, sheep, fences, and timber, all gone, and the "chub" with them. . . .

Before this storm the beach opposite the Island consisted of high sand hills and ridges. The height of these ridges had greatly increased since the War of 1812. This I ascertained from the following facts. This storm tide had cut these ridges away and in their stead, at a certain point on the beach, appeared, to the great wonder of the young, a large thicket of dead cedars, whose gigantic arms stretched impressively heavenward.

Uncle Johnny Beasley knew all about these cedars, for he had boiled salt under these trees in the War of 1812; their thick foliage had screened him and others from the view of the British as they passed up and down the coast.

He said that he had left his salt pans there; they had been sanded up and the cedars with them; now he could get them. He got some help and went over, the writer and his father along with them. He pointed out an old stooping cedar upon which he had sat when boiling salt, and pointed out the place of the pans. Two of the pans three by six feet and ten inches deep, were found a little below the surface. He carried them home after they had been buried over thirty years. . . .

On the 8th day of September, of the same year, another

A HISTORIAN'S COAST

The rescue party discovered Cooper's house abandoned and drifting in a copse of live oaks. "Over to Bowden's they went," Ansell recounted, "and found his house anchored and tied to the surrounding live oaks, tumbling about, but being kept on its balance by many devices." The Coopers and Bowdens were crowded into a rooftop garret. Salt water lapped at the joists just below them.

The panicked families boarded the fishing boat and were removed to Knotts Island. Nobody would live on that part of Currituck Banks again for many years.

The nor'easter of 1846 affected Knotts Island's ecology long after the debris was cleared, the dead livestock buried, and the homes repaired. For one thing, the freshwater bay between Knotts

storm arose. It was said, it blew stronger than the previous one, and would have done the same damage, if there had been anything left to damage. The few cattle and hogs put on the marshes and beach from the high land and gotten during Summer from elsewhere were swept away as before. This storm had the same staying quality as the former one, and blew with more force, but the wind ranged farther north, consequently the tide lacked about two feet being as high as it was in the former storm. Also, the former was in spring-tide the latter in neap-tide; so said the believers in lunar influences.

The Sound, and especially the Island bay, kept salt and saltish for years thereafter, so much so, that small oysters were formed along the bay shore.

Schools of porpoise promenaded daily the Island Channel and many kinds of saltwater fish were abundant.

The day before the night this storm set in, I caught six flying fish with hook and line, the first I had ever seen.

John Ansell, larger than myself, was with me. We tried the Island sloughs and channel and did not get a bite. We then decided to stem the head wind to Martin's Point slough by the beach where fish were generally found. To do this we had to cross a great shoal the depth of which ranged from one to two feet of water. After low tides small boats would have to be pulled over this shoal. The tide at this time was about two feet.

In crossing this shoal we saw that the water was very thickly stirred by something; not only was this unusual, but we had never seen that hard, clear-bottomed sand bar in such commotion before; further, who ever saw fish on this hard sand shoal, except occasionally a mullet? John said this stir was caused by fish. We bored a pole down into this hard bottom, and tied our boat.

We found the water teeming with fish, and such biting we had never enjoyed before. We soon caught more than enough, and then played with the fish for fun. We soon dispensed with the bait for it was not needed. We could draw our hooks swiftly through the water and hook them in all manner of ways and bring them in. While using bait John caught two in one draw—one in the mouth, where the hook protruded out far enough to hang the other in its abdominal regions.

The fish were so numerous on that shoal you would seldom miss one in drawing the hook through the water. This fish swarm was the fore-runner of that swiftly approaching storm.

From Henry Beasley Ansell,
"Recollections of a Life Time and More" (circa 1907)
Unpublished manuscript at the
Southern Historical Collection,
University of North Carolina at Chapel Hill.

Henry Ansell's Recollections of Knotts Island

Island and Currituck Banks turned salty again, damaging the waterfowl feeding grounds and interrupting the freshwater fishing on which Knotts Islanders had come to rely. Dolphins, stingrays, and small oysters even returned to local waters for a few years.

Great Marsh Bay, the freshwater marsh that separates Knotts Island from the mainland of Currituck County, suffered a different fate. Flooded by salt water, the freshwater grasses died off, and the bay was left, in Ansell's words, "in drift, mire, mud, and slime." The brackish pools of muddy water made an ideal breeding ground for mosquitoes. For years, Knotts Islanders cursed Great Marsh Bay's flooding for a plague of mosquito bites and mosquito-borne diseases.

Knotts Islanders did not realize the nor'easter's greatest damage until the summer of 1846. Ever since much of the island had been deforested in the eighteenth century for fuel and naval stores, they had relied on longleaf pine timber from a vast, swampy tract of Great Marsh Bay. "When it came time for these trees to commence their summer's growth, they died," recalled Ansell, "together with all the firewood and rail timber on the adjacent knolls."

Six decades later, Ansell was still mourning the storm's destruction of the longleaf pine forest: "From this loss the island to this day has not recovered, nor can it ever recover. This timber . . . grew scarcer and scarcer as the years rolled on, and at present little can be found."

Out on Currituck Banks, the nor'easter had flattened the sand dunes and ridges. From beneath the sand appeared, "to the great wonder of the young, a large thicket of dead cedars, whose gigantic arms stretched impressively heaven-ward," Ansell remembered. (Such "ghost forests" are caused by wind-driven dunes that migrate over maritime forests.) Ansell's uncle Johnny Beasley had boiled salt under the boughs of those same cedars during the War of 1812, screened from the view of the British ships by their thick foliage. After the storm, Beasley recovered salt pans that had been buried by sand for thirty years. Other islanders dug out the ghost cedars and sold them for vessel timbers.

Things only got worse that fall. Another storm, a vicious hurricane, hit Knotts Island in September 1846. Best remembered today for opening Hatteras and Oregon Inlets, the hurricane struck Knotts Island when gardens and fields were brimming with produce. According to Ansell, the few hogs and cattle left after the nor'easter "were swept away as before." Many families must have gone hungry that winter.

I thought about Ansell and the nor'easter of 1846 as I left Great Marsh. Until Hurricanes

Bertha and Fran in 1996, many of us had forgotten how sudden, cataclysmic forces shape our coast. Mountains are pushed upward with staggering patience by slow tectonic grinding, an inch or two a year, until they reach the sky. But that has never been our coast's way of doing things. Disaster and upheaval are its lifeblood, just as much as sand and salt water. Ansell learned that lesson 150 years ago, and it is a lesson best not forgotten.

A cool drizzle descended on the state ferry back to the mainland. For a long time, I stood at the stern and watched the distant, crowded lights at Currituck Banks. That horizon would have been pitch dark a few years ago. But these days, it glows with condos, shopping centers, and movie stars' homes. I could not help thinking that somewhere out in the North Atlantic, a nor'easter is waiting to be born, a storm that will rival the one in 1846. It may hit Currituck Banks next year, in 10 years, or in 150 years. But sooner or later, that sky will once again be just as dark as the night Ansell heard the Atlantic's waves pounding the shores of Knotts Island.

Collecting the crude turpentine
North Carolina Division of Archives and History

A Historian's Coast

THE RISE AND FALL
OF THE RICH LANDS

Recently, I walked across the former site of the Rich Lands Plantation in Onslow County, a shining jewel in the naval stores industry of the Old South. John Avirett and more than 125 slaves built a kingdom out of longleaf pines' resin, producing vast quantities of turpentine, tar, pitch, and rosin. Long gone, the Rich Lands once sprawled across more than twenty-two thousand acres just east of what is now the town of Richlands, between Kenansville and Jacksonville.

With the help of Dennis Jones, a local historian and educator, I went in search of the Rich Lands' former glory. Poking around the piney woods, we found circular imprints of old tar pits still scarring the earth. Dennis showed me a thick layer of rosin residue by the banks of Catherine Lake, the former site of Avirett's turpentine distilleries. He also pointed out an old rice dam and a well-chiseled marl bed, once a source of lime for the plantation's fields. Toward dusk, he led me to Alum Spring, which rises out of a gaping limestone rift. Now in deep forest, the spring was a popular picnic spot for some of the wealthiest planters in North Carolina. Finally, Dennis showed me the way to the Avirett family's cemetery. It was only a few graves surrounded by a crumbling brick wall tangled in trumpet vine. Not far off, we barely made out the low spot where the Rich Lands' slaves are said to have buried their dead.

Dennis and I recognized these landmarks because James Battle Avirett, John's son, wrote an extraordinary memoir of growing up at the Rich

Lands. Published in 1901, *The Old Plantation: How We Lived in Great House and Cabin before the War* is an unparalleled account of the turpentine boom days in the Old South—the days that made North Carolina the Tar Heel State. After reading Avirett's memoir, you can practically see the Rich Lands as it was 150 years ago: the fine manor house, the slave quarters, the distilleries, the picnic grounds at Alum Spring, and the great piney woods itself. No aspect of social life or turpentining at the Rich Lands seems to have escaped him.

Yet Avirett did not tell all. I discovered that behind *The Old Plantation* is an untold saga, a mystery far more intriguing than the book itself. In reality, Avirett's flattering portrait of the Rich Lands conceals a stunning tale of ecological ruin and personal tragedy. It is a story of nostalgia and deceit that goes to the heart of how we remember the Old South today.

The longleaf pine (*Palus palustris*) once defined the American South as distinctively as the tallgrass prairie set apart the Great Plains. The longleaf forest covered 130 million acres in a hundred-mile swath from Tidewater Virginia to eastern Texas. Carolina colonists distilled the longleafs' crude resin (turpentine) into "spirits of turpentine" and rosin, and they produced tar and pitch by smoldering longleaf wood in earthen kilns. These products were known as "naval stores" because they played a critical role in caulking wooden ships and preserving their hemp lines.

By 1840, North Carolina produced 96 percent of the turpentine, tar, and rosin in the United States. The vast majority came from twelve tidewater counties, including John Avirett's Onslow County. At that time, Wilmington exported more naval stores than any other port in the world. After prices rose steeply with the removal of British duties on American turpentine in 1846, Wilmington doubled in population and became the state's largest city.

New uses for turpentine as a solvent, paint ingredient, and illuminant raised the naval stores industry to even greater heights. The number of distilleries in Wilmington skyrocketed from two in 1841 to more than twenty in 1852; up the Cape Fear River, the number of turpentine distilleries in Fayetteville climbed from one to thirty-two. Naval stores became the third most important agricultural commodity produced in the South, exceeded by only cotton and tobacco.

The Aviretts stood at the pinnacle of naval stores society. An Avirett of German Huguenot descent had settled in Onslow County by 1747. The family grew prosperous enough by 1791 to host President George Washington during his Southern tour. John Alfred Avirett, born in or around 1797, gradually built a turpentine empire

TURPENTINE BARRELS ON WATER STREET, WILMINGTON, NORTH CAROLINA, 1873
North Carolina Division of Archives and History

that included a 20,000-acre longleaf orchard, 125 slaves, and a magnificent three-story manor house. He was also the Onslow County sheriff for two decades.

His son James, the author of *The Old Plantation*, was born at the Rich Lands in 1835. James became an Episcopal priest and served as a Confederate chaplain during the Civil War. After Appomattox, he directed a Virginia seminary. He was later rector for several churches in New York. When he returned to North Carolina in 1894, James often spoke at Confederate soldiers' reunions, where he extolled the virtues of antebellum life at the Rich Lands. Before he died in 1912, he gained a measure of fame for reputedly being the oldest living Confederate chaplain.

In *The Old Plantation*, James Avirett vividly recalled the making of naval stores at the Rich Lands. It occurred in a world unto itself. The piney woods—or turpentine orchard—ran all the way from the New River to the White Oak pocosin. The distilling center was located at Catherine Lake, about three miles from the main house. It included two distilleries, mule stables, barracks, storage sheds, a windmill, and cooperage shops and a glue house for making barrels.

An older slave named Philip oversaw the production of about thirty thousand barrels of turpentine a year. He was second in command to John Avirett himself in managing the Rich Lands. James Avirett described Philip as "very little, if any, inferior to any man, white or colored." His father consulted with Philip nightly about the plantation's business, and Philip presented a full accounting of the week's progress to his master every Saturday morning. Avirett admitted that without Philip, his father "would have been sadly at sea."

Turpentining began every year by burning away the undergrowth in the pine forest to open the woods to slave laborers. In the late fall and winter, twenty-five to thirty axmen cut "boxes"— shallow, **V**-shaped incisions in the bark—that exposed the pine sap and directed it down to a single point. There, the workers hewed a small bowl capable of holding about a quart of raw turpentine. Using long iron blades called "roundshaves," the axmen kept the sap flowing into the bowls all summer by periodically chipping away dried sap.

Slaves next moved with dippers through the pines to collect the turpentine out of the boxes and empty it into barrels scattered about the woods. Draymen carried the barrels in mule carts to Catherine Lake, where a slave named Harry oversaw the distilling, an art every bit as sophisticated as making good bourbon.

The success of the naval stores industry relied on slave skills, but James Avirett admitted that

A TURPENTINE CAMP IN NORTH CAROLINA
North Carolina Division of Archives and History

"The Turpentine Orchards"

Catherine Lake was the largest of a chain of seven or eight small lakes which we find in the midst of the twenty-two thousand acres of splendid pine trees embracing the turpentine orchards of this estate. This lake was about a half mile in length and from a quarter to three-eighths of a mile in breadth, in many places quite deep and in some places covered over with the pads of water lilies, in season very beautiful with their large white flowers. There was neither visible outlet nor inlet. It must have derived its bountiful and uniform supply of crystal water from hidden springs. . . .

From yonder little island we will get a full view of the old planter's possessions on the south bank of this lake, and we will have a long, long talk about this branch of the plantation industries. . . .

As compared with the other staples of the South, what do you regard as the most serious drawback or disadvantage of the planter's turpentine interests? The laborers, and notably so the chippers, are employed in large, wooded tracts of country, out of range of anything like close oversight and must be stimulated to their best work, as well by premiums for best crops as by so regulating their work that a portion of each week is their own to do as they please with. It is different on the cotton, sugar, tobacco and rice plantations. The great disadvantage in the crop, however, is that the distilleries, the spirits of turpentine, the resin, and in fine the whole plant and its yields are so combustible that no insurance company, domestic or foreign, will insure the property. The only protection against fire that can be had is to police the premises as thoroughly as possible. How is this done? By placing here and there all over the orchards double log cabins for the families of some twenty or more white men.

These people occupy these cabins free of rent, with as much land as they choose to cultivate, which rarely extends beyond a garden and truck patch, the men fishing and hunting by day and night, while the women hoe the little crops and raise poultry, the children gathering whortleberries and wild currants. These men are required to do three things; first, they are to guard the orchards from fire, and if a small fire occur, as it often does in the summer time by lightning striking and igniting a resinous pine tree, they and their families must extinguish it. If it gets beyond their control they are to blow horns, summon the neighboring tenants and, sending all around for help, fight the fire fiend until it is put out; secondly, they must once a week salt and care for the herd of cattle and drove of sheep belonging to the proprietor, carefully penning the sheep at night so as to protect them from the dogs, wildcats and bears, which are found in those large tracts of unbroken forests. Thirdly, they must look out for the planter's honey bees, and when the cold weather sets in they must take the honey and carry it into the mansion for the use of the planter's family.

From James B. Avirett,
The Old Plantation: How We Lived in Great House and Cabin before the War
(New York: F. Tennyson Neely Company, 1901)

"close surveillance" of the slave work force was simply impossible. Unlike slaves on other Southern plantations, turpentine workers ranged over hundreds of acres of remote woodlands. Working alone or in pairs, they stayed in primitive camps with little oversight during boxing, chipping, and collecting. The work was arduous, the heat unbearable, the housing squalid, the insects a scourge.

Yet compared to other slaves, naval stores workers had certain blessings. Since John Avirett could not keep an eye on forest workers, he tried to spur them "to their best work" by paying rewards if they exceeded his quotas for boxing, chipping, and barrel making. Thus, they had money to spend at a store located at Philip's cabin and, to John Avirett's dismay, in the black market that thrived on the plantation's outskirts. The slaves must also have relished their independent life in the piney woods.

Now, we come to the grave—and telling—deception at the heart of *The Old Plantation*. James Avirett credited the naval stores industry with building the Rich Lands, but he refused to acknowledge that it was also his family's downfall. *The Old Plantation* portrayed the Rich Lands as an idyllic paradise (think *Gone with the Wind* and Tara here) right up until the Civil War. He bitterly blamed that horrible war and the freeing of the slaves for destroying the Rich Lands.

In reality, the Civil War had nothing to do with its ruin. From Onslow County records, I discovered that an ecological donnybrook—the destruction of the longleaf forest—brought down both the Rich Lands and the Avirett family in 1857, four years *before* the Civil War.

In the 1840s and 1850s, the naval stores industry was rapidly destroying the longleaf pine forest throughout tidewater North Carolina. James Avirett did not mention deforestation in *The Old Plantation*, but contemporary travelers often commented, in the words of one, on seeing "nothing but Pinewoods . . . on whose trees the process of gumming turpentine was visible." The famed agriculturist Edmund Ruffin, a friend of the Averitts, observed that "scarcely a good [longleaf] in North Carolina has escaped that operation."

The average lifetime of longleafs after boxing was only about six years. According to G. Terry Sharrer, a Smithsonian forestry historian, 100 gallons of turpentine were the product of 12 to 14 acres of longleaf forest. When Wilmington's exports rose from 7,218 barrels in 1847 to more than 120,000 a decade later, every 50,000-barrel increase came at the expense of another 250,000 acres of piney woods. Even turpentine orchards as large as the Rich Lands eventually succumbed to ax and roundshave.

Since they had heavy investments in slaves and land, planters such as the Aviretts rushed to box new longleaf stands during the turpentine boom. It was a self-destructive spiral downward. Many planters reportedly collected only the first season's pine sap—the so-called virgin dip—because it earned the highest price. High winds, disease, and pine beetles ravaged the weakened trees. And controlled burns and free-grazing hogs consumed young seedlings, depriving the forest of a chance to regenerate.

Confronted by dying forests, many turpentiners abandoned North Carolina. They shifted the naval stores industry's center to the pine barrens of South Carolina and Georgia, then to the uplands of Alabama, Mississippi, and Louisiana, and finally to eastern Texas. Depression hit the piney woods of Onslow County, and the population plummeted 30 percent between 1820 and 1860. Many of John Avirett's closest friends pulled up stakes and moved to Wilmington and other towns. They survived by diversifying into railroads, shipping, and banking. Avirett did not. He was a man of the earth, and he clung tenaciously—and fatally—to the Rich Lands.

Personal tragedy hastened his downfall. In February 1851, the Rich Lands manor house burned to the ground. Not long after, he lost two daughters during childbirth. The fresh graves and

A TURPENTINER IN CUMBERLAND COUNTY, N.C. , CIRCA 1860
North Carolina Division of Archives and History

dead longleafs must have made the Rich Lands seem like a cursed place in the 1850s. Yet only nostalgia for James Avirett's boyhood home and the Old South, and not a word of these tragedies, is found in *The Old Plantation*.

The final straw came in 1857. John Avirett, by then a pitiable figure, sold the family's new house and ten thousand acres for twenty-five thousand dollars. He abdicated another ten thousand acres "together with the turpentine distilleries and fixtures" for twenty thousand dollars. He must have been deeply in debt. Not only did he sell

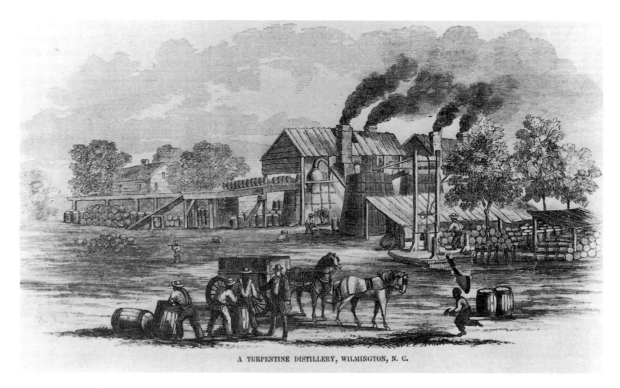

A TURPENTINE DISTILLERY IN WILMINGTON, NORTH CAROLINA, 1873
North Carolina Division of Archives and History

the homeplace and ancestral graveyard, but he soon relocated to Goldsboro, where he was virtually penniless by 1860. He seems to have died in or around 1863. Local legend says that he perished in a poorhouse or insane asylum.

I have returned to the Rich Lands often since Dennis Jones first shared its secrets with me. I like to walk to Alum Spring, a quiet, restful spot. When I am there, I often wonder why James Avirett blamed the Civil War for his family's ruin. I imagine that he never recovered from the shock of losing the Rich Lands in 1857. He had to blame some power greater than a dwindling forest. But I also suspect that Avirett wanted to glorify his father and all the old Southern planters. He wanted, most of all, to help the world forget what they had done to the South.

THE BOOK OF NATURE

I n 1895, a popcorn peddler named Allen Parker told the story of his life as a slave on the North Carolina coast. Parker published only a few copies of *Recollections of Slavery Times* for his friends and family in Worcester, Massachusetts, where he lived after the Civil War. The slim, ninety-seven-page book quickly faded into obscurity, remaining unknown even to the leading scholars on American slave narratives.

Then, two or three years ago, I stumbled upon a copy of this priceless lost memoir at the Illinois State Historical Library in Springfield, Illinois. How the book ended up in Illinois remains a mystery. But that manuscript turned out to be the only surviving copy of Parker's *Recollections* in any library or archive in the United States. As yet, I have found no evidence that any other copies have survived.

I do not know if I can put into words the excitement, almost the sheer joy, that a historian feels at discovering a document like Parker's *Recollections*. I know it sounds, well, weird, but I find these discoveries just as exhilarating as paddling into a swamp wilderness or exploring a remote barrier island after a big storm. A whole new world opens up before you, and you never know what wonders and surprises will be revealed in that uncharted territory.

For me, this may be especially true of a slave narrative like Parker's *Recollections*. As I travel along the coast, I rarely find any trace of its slave past. Though African American slaves once made up a majority of the population in many tidewater towns and counties, they are virtually invisible in the historic sites, museums, monuments, and markers that portray coastal life before 1865. When Parker decried the fate of his mother, he described that of all slaves who lived and died in coastal North Carolina. In his words, she "now lies buried in an unmarked and neglected grave."

The scarcity of firsthand accounts of slavery is one important stumbling block to studying slave life. Slaves could not legally be taught to read and write, so they left few written records. To piece together their lives, historians have had to rely almost entirely on accounts left by their masters. The result has been both a planter-centered view of slave life and a fragmented portrait of the antebellum past in general.

To appreciate the importance of a newly discovered slave narrative like Parker's *Recollections*, we only have to remember that merely a half-dozen other slave writings are known to have arisen from tidewater North Carolina. Between 1843 and 1852, Harriet Jacobs of Edenton, Moses Grandy of Camden County, and Thomas H. Jones of Wilmington published autobiographies after escaping from the South. *Incidents in the Life of a Slave Girl*, Jacobs's narrative, has been belatedly recognized as a classic of American literature. In addition, William H. Robinson of Wilmington, Wil-liam Ferebee

(once a Currituck slave waterman), and William Henry Singleton (a slave at Garbacon Creek in what is now Carteret County, then part of Craven County) all published memoirs after the Civil War. Except for Jacobs's *Incidents* and Singleton's *Recollections of My Slavery Days*, these slave narratives can be found only in the largest university libraries and are not readily available to the general public.

But Parker's *Recollections* is exciting not only because it is such a rare document. It offers insights into tidewater life—and not just slave life—that cannot be found anywhere else. Parker worked for a great variety of small planters and yeoman farmers, including the poor sort of backwoods farmer who barely scratched out a living on the edge of the Great Dismal Swamp. This is a part of Albemarle society long overshadowed by the great planters and wealthy merchants whose family records we have inherited and whose homes are preserved in historic districts. Better than any source I have ever seen, Parker's memoir cuts through that thin upper crust of Albemarle society and lets us see into the heart of daily life for black and white, slave and free.

Allen Parker's story begins in Chowan County over a century and a half ago. Born about 1840, he was the son of slaves Millie Parker and Jeff Ellick. He lived on a modest plantation owned

PURVIS SLAVE CABIN IN GREENE COUNTY, ONE OF THE LAST SURVIVING SLAVE CABINS IN NORTH CAROLINA
North Carolina Museum of History

by Peter Parker in the Chowan community, a rural neighborhood located eight miles north of Edenton (then the largest seaport on Albemarle Sound) and bordered by Bear Swamp, the Great Dismal Swamp, and two blackwater rivers, the Chowan and the Yeopim. "The country around Chowan was not very thickly settled," Parker wrote in *Recollections*, "the land being divided up into farms or plantations, upon which was raised wheat, Indian corn, rye, oats, peanuts, sweet-potatoes and sometimes rice."

Peter Parker died when Allen was a baby. He left the slave boy and his mother to his infant daughter, Annie, with the stipulation that Millie and Allen should be "hired out" by her guardian until she was an adult. The guardian basically auctioned off the slaves to other individuals for a year at a time. The hirers got the slaves' labor; Peter Parker's estate got the proceeds; Millie and Allen were supposed to get food and clothing. Like many slaves in the Albemarle Sound vicinity, Allen Parker thus moved annually from master to master.

He never labored for truly prosperous planters, but at times, he was leased to relatively wealthy men. Darias White, for instance, employed forty slave loggers and teams of mules and oxen in a local swamp, where they harvested old-growth hardwoods for shipbuilding timbers. More often,

HEYWOOD DIXON, SLAVE CARPENTER IN GREENE COUNTY, NORTH CAROLINA, CIRCA 1855 – 1860. THIS IS ONE OF THE FEW SURVIVING IMAGES OF A SLAVE IN NORTH CAROLINA.
North Carolina Division of Archives and History

Parker worked for one-mule farmers who could not afford to own a slave or even to hire slaves except after exceptionally good harvests.

During his childhood, Allen Parker lived among several "good masters," hardworking men with whose families he shared a dinner table. Within the boundaries of his enslavement, these masters treated him decently. He had a special fondness for a small farmer and storekeeper named George Williams, recalling that he played with Williams's children and learned some of their school lessons: "I had many good times playing with the other children[,] for whatever the grown white people might think about the colored people, the little children did not know any difference when they were allowed to play with the slave children."

Young Parker also worked for brutal, malevolent masters who beat him, kept him hungry, and tried at every turn to subdue his spirit. A farmer named Small was among the worst. He beat Allen's mother severely and worked her day and night in the fields and in his kitchen while she was still breast-feeding a new baby. Confronted with men so vile, Allen and his mother ran away several times, seeking refuge with other slaves or white friends.

When the Civil War broke out, Parker was among the thousands of slaves who escaped from tidewater plantations to Union territory. The Union army captured the Outer Banks and most of the state's seaports by early 1862, and Albemarle slaves staged a colossal boatlift to freedom behind Union lines. While other Albemarle slaves confiscated sloops or built makeshift rafts and sailed to Union outposts as far away as Roanoke Island and the Outer Banks, Parker did not have to travel so far. He rowed out to a Union gunboat that had come up the Chowan River.

During the Federal occupation, Parker served in the Union navy in the North Carolina sounds. He later worked at a Beaufort sawmill before departing the South as a merchant sailor. He eventually settled in Worcester, Massachusetts, where he married and raised a family while working as a street peddler.

Recollections of Slavery Times may be most important for describing the daily rhythms of slave life in the Carolina tidewater. Parker neither neglects nor lingers over slavery's terrors. Instead, his genius is in chronicling the details of daily life. He spends four pages simply describing a typical slave cabin—its construction; the composition of its beams, mortar, roof, chimney, doors, and windows; even the cooking utensils and furniture within it.

Parker is like that with everything, and it is this accretion of ordinary details—his diet, clothing, pastimes, religion, music, family—that allows him to distill an essence of slavery far more telling than a litany of atrocities alone.

Parker had a special awareness of the ways in which his masters relied on African American knowledge of agriculture and the earth. My colleague Peter Wood has documented how West African slaves introduced rice cultivation into the Low Country of South Carolina, a critical step in colonizing the tidewater there and along the Lower Cape Fear. Today's historians share a growing appreciation for the West African roots of agriculture in the early South.

But Parker seems to be making a broader argument. He is not merely saying that slaves brought their know-how of West African crops to the Americas, but also that they gleaned new lessons out of the American woods, fields, and waters simply because they worked in them and relied on them far more extensively than did their masters.

"Being out of doors a great deal of the time, and having no books, [we slaves] learned many things from the book of Nature, which were unknown to white people, notwithstanding their knowledge of books," Parker wrote. "And it often happened that the master would be guided by the slave as to the proper time to plant his corn, sow his grain, or harvest his crops, and many things of this kind, which were to the master a source of care and anxiety, seemed to come to the slave as it were by instinct and not often did they make a mistake in their prophecies."

This reliance on slaves and their knowledge of the "book of Nature" is scarcely surprising. The men and women who toiled in fields of cotton, tobacco, wheat, and corn day in and day out, year after year, became intimately acquainted with every aspect of cultivation: clearing land, fertilizing, ditching, sowing, weeding, harvesting, selecting new seed for the next crop. Overseers came

and went, and planters were often diverted by other business interests, but slaves got their hands dirty sunup to sundown every day—and learned the lessons that the earth had to offer.

Parker must have learned a great deal about nature when he worked at Darias White's timber camp near the Great Dismal Swamp. There, he drove oxen teams that hauled hundred-foot-long logs out of the swamp to blackwater streams where they could be floated to a sawmill. "I liked this sort of work very well as it was not often hard, and there was a great deal of excitement about it," he remembered.

That year, Parker was among approximately forty slaves who, he wrote, "camped in the woods through the entire lumber season." They lived in a camp "made of logs, bark and pieces of board, which would enclose the camp on three sides, [and] on the fourth a large fire would be built at night." This sort of camp life is not our usual image of slavery, but it was very common in the timber, shingle-making, and naval stores industries. Slaves like Parker developed a unique knowledge of the forest ecology from spending months in such camps.

Whether in swamp or field, the slaves were intimately bound to the "book of Nature." They related to nature in a way that was different from their masters. Take, for instance, the ways master and slave measured the passage of time. Planters told time with watches and clocks. "The slaves," Parker wrote, "were obliged to depend upon the sun, moon, and stars and other things in nature."

Of course, Parker and his enslaved brethren did not utilize their familiarity with the "book of Nature" only to raise their masters' crops and cut their timber. They frequently employed the same knowledge to weaken the grip of bondage on their lives. The slaves depended upon by the planters for their knowledge of agriculture, fishing, and forest industries thus achieved at least a small shift in their favor in the never-ending power struggle between master and slave.

Just as they learned to rely on the moon and stars in the absence of mechanical clocks, so Albemarle slaves looked in ingenious ways to their natural environment to improve and vary their food rations—and gain a small but important foothold outside their masters' households. Parker described, for instance, how slaves turned pine needles and small twigs into tea and made coffee out of burnt corn and wheat.

Albemarle slaves also enriched their diets with wild game. "Night," Parker wrote, "was the slave's holiday." It was no accident that he devoted a long chapter of *Recollections* to how slaves hunted raccoons, opossums, and other nocturnal game. "The slaves believed that the wild game was intended for them," he observed, "for while the master was enjoying his roast beef or lamb, he did not think that his slaves needed anything of the sort."

Sometimes, the slaves' game was not quite as wild as raccoons and opossums. Tidewater farmers allowed their hogs to graze freely in the woods, where they lived cheaply off acorns and roots until rounded up for slaughter. Multitudes of these hogs lived in coastal woodlands, and their rapacious grazing habits contributed to the forests' parklike appearance, upon which visitors so often remarked. Many hogs grew quite wild over the generations and closely resembled wild boars.

Runaway slaves relied heavily on feral hogs,

but Parker pointed out that they were also important to plantation workers still in bondage. One of his harshest taskmasters was a farmer named Elisha Buck. "He did not treat us at all well," Parker noted, "and it was not often that we had all we wanted to eat." Buck caught and whipped Parker and another slave the first time that they killed a free-grazing hog.

"It did not do much good to either of us," recalled Parker, "for on the following Sunday I went into the woods again and got another pig which I dressed in the night." He realized that there were many poor whites quite willing to take advantage of a neighboring planter's hogs so long as a slave took the risk for them.

"As I did not have every advantage of a first-class slaughter house I was obliged to manage as best I could," Parker wrote. "Accordingly I built a fire and gave the pig a good singeing and while he was warm from the effects of the fire. I put him into water, and then scraped him with a case-knife and finally got him clean.

"When he was properly dressed," he continued, "I carried him on my shoulder about three miles, and turned him over to a 'poor white' who took him to a neighboring town the next day, and sold him for me. I got back to quarters before the hands were called in the morning so that no one knew where I had been.

"In due time the 'poor white' gave me my share

"Many of the Slaves Camped in the Woods"

Sometime in the 1850s, Allen Parker was hired out to haul lumber from local swamps, a job that gave him greater liberty and more decent treatment than he had received on the small farms and plantations where he worked previously.

The following year after I left Cofell I went to work for Darias White who was a step son of my old master, and I continued to work for him three years. His business was to get out oak and hard pine lumber most of which was used in ship-building.

All the time I worked for White I drove team, and had charge of the mules and one horse. The horse was kept by my master for his own use. The mules were used entirely for teaming. Besides these he had a large number of oxen that were used for hawling the great logs out of the woods.

These logs were of the largest kind and were often one hundred feet or more in length. The but end of the log was fastened to the axletree of an enormous pair of wheels, from the axletree projected a long tongue, to which was attached a single yoke of oxen. In front of this yoke of oxen there was sometimes as many as fifteen yoke of oxen one ahead of the other and all fastened by a chain to the end of the tongue. A team of this kind required about eight drivers. Each driver was seated on the yoke of one pair of oxen, and would drive that yoke and the yoke in front.

Instead of a whip such as is used in the north, the drivers would have a long slender birch rod, which when green would be almost as durable as a raw-hide.

DRAWING OF A RUNAWAY SLAVE AND HIS AFRICAN AMERICAN ALLY IN A COASTAL SWAMP
North Carolina Division of Archives and History

The small end of the log was also hung between a large pair of wheels. To the tongue of which was fastened a rope from twelve to fifteen feet long with a knot in the end. The end of this rope was given into the hands of a strong active negro, whose business it was to steer the logs. When everything was ready the word to start would be given and away the logs went, the oxen pulling with all their might and the log drivers shouting at the top of their voices.

The man with the guiding ropes of the rear wheels [was] sometimes on the logs[,] sometimes on the ground at one side, and sometimes at the other side working with all his strength to keep the log in its place, and so the procession proceeded from the woods to the river bank, where the log would be left till enough were got together to ship to market.

Very often I had to drive oxen myself, though my business generally was to drive the mules, drawing grain and fodder for the oxen. Sometimes the mules would be hitched in front of the ox team. I liked this sort of work very well as it was not often hard, and there was a good deal of excitement to it. . . .

Many of the slaves camped in the woods through the entire lumber season.

A camp would be made of logs, bark and pieces of board, which would enclose the camp on three sides, [and] on the fourth a large fire would be built at night, at which we did our cooking. Every evening after supper had been disposed of the slaves would spend the time till bed time in singing and telling stories.

From Allen Parker,
Recollections of Slavery Times (1895)

of the money he got for the pig. With this money I bought some cloth, which a white woman made into a coat and a pair of pants for me."

Many planters allowed slaves to keep vegetable and herb gardens around their cabins, so long as they tended them only in their spare time. Other slaves clandestinely trapped, fished, and gardened in the wild, keeping the fruits of their labor for their own tables or, like Parker with his hog, trading them with poor whites nearby. A desire for more varied, healthier diets led slaves whenever possible into their own gardens, into the forest, and on to the rivers and sounds.

Parker also wrote of how slaves relied on the "book of Nature" in a way that went beyond simple knowledge of the land to a more personal relationship with, and even communication with, the natural world. Parker remembered, for instance,

how slaves used the subtle variations in owls' calls to take heed of the approach of their masters, which enabled them to hide successfully or to labor clandestinely for their own gain. "The slaves not only believed that the owl was their friend, and that his language was intended entirely for them, but also believed that his language was not understood by the white folks," he recalled.

According to Parker, Albemarle slaves found meaning in all sorts of natural signs. "A cloud over the moon, a rainy night, the barking of a dog, or any other circumstance [that] seemed to aid them in carrying out their plans, they thought that it was intended especially for their benefit," he wrote.

I suppose this sense that nature was on their side might arise in any oppressed people living off the land. But I also wonder if, to some degree, this conviction originated in a theological outlook prevalent among the Ba-Kongo, Igbo, Asante, and many other West African peoples imported to the Americas. Their religious backgrounds were very different, but most did share a world view in which the dead—the ancestors—played an active role in the affairs of the living. Many believed that the ancestors sometimes expressed themselves through wild animals and natural events. Most also believed in lesser deities, or spirits, that were keepers of rivers, forests, and other wild places, which further imparted a sacred character to nature.

I do not know how deeply the attitudes of Albemarle slaves toward nature embodied African spiritual beliefs. Certainly, I have observed an intimate communion with coastal lands among the most knowledgeable of the old-timers—black, white, and red—with whom I have had the privilege of exploring swamps and forests. Nevertheless, when I read through Allen Parker's *Recollections*, I am drawn again and again to the almost sacred attitude that Albemarle slaves displayed toward the natural world. And at such times, I wonder if in those pages we might have far more to learn than I ever expected, and not just about the past.

Elliott Coues, surgeon, U. S. Army

This photograph was made in 1864 when Coues was first commissioned in the Army.

From Bird-Lore, *January-February, 1902*

ELLIOTT COUES:
A NATURALIST
AT FORT MACON

In February 1869, a United States Army surgeon named Elliott Coues began a two-year tour of duty at Fort Macon. Destined to become the foremost American ornithologist of his day, the young Coues (pronounced "Cows") resented being sent to the sandy, remote, and wind-swept eastern end of Bogue Banks, where the old fort guarded Beaufort Inlet. He called it a "detestable place" and said he "always felt it a sort of vague disgrace" that the army had exiled him so far from the Smithsonian Institution and the nation's other centers for the study of natural history, Boston and Philadelphia.

Yet Coues made the most of his stint at Fort Macon. Bogue Banks, he had to admit, was a "good place for field natural history." He did ex-haustive studies of shorebirds, marsh birds, and seabirds but hardly confined his curiosity to winged creatures. By the time he left in November 1870, Coues had conducted one of the most thorough surveys of animal life ever undertaken anywhere on the southeastern coast of North America. He published it in a weighty five-part series in the *Proceedings of the Academy of Natural Sciences of Philadelphia*.

Born September 9, 1842, in Portsmouth, New Hampshire, Coues was a protégé of Spencer Baird, the founder of the Smithsonian Institution. He hoped to join his mentor in Washington, D.C., after fieldwork in Arizona and South Carolina. But like many nineteenth-century naturalists who were not independently wealthy, he found an army medical career his only real chance to see the world and make a name for himself. He earned his medical degree at Columbia University in 1863 and stayed in the army for seventeen years.

Coues was a prolific writer. While in the army, he published three hundred articles and papers, and he later wrote several landmark texts of natural history. While his far-ranging curiosity led him down some rather eclectic paths—his thousand-page *Monographs of North American Rodentia*, cowritten with Joel Asaph Allen in 1877, comes to mind—Coues gained the greatest acclaim for his *Hand-book of Field and General Ornithology* (1890) and *Key to North American Birds* (1903), two classics renowned for their accuracy and Coues's meticulous illustrations.

When Coues and his wife moved to North Carolina in 1869, some 125 enlisted men lived within Fort Macon. Married soldiers resided in six wooden barracks nearby. In an 1870 report for the United States surgeon general's office, Coues wrote that the fort was overcrowded, moldy, lacking in proper sanitary facilities, and exposed to "shifting winds" that "wafted malaria from the

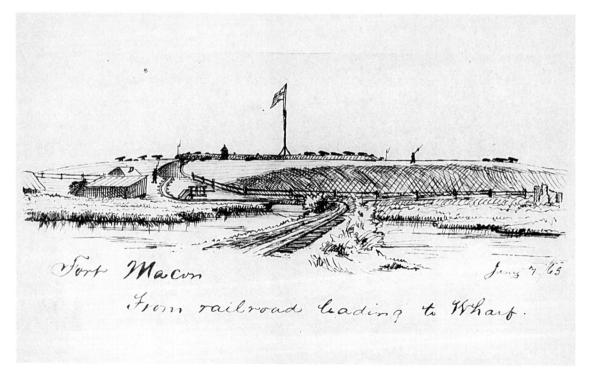

A UNION SOLDIER'S SKETCH OF FORT MACON IN 1863
North Carolina Division of Archives and History

swamps of the mainland." He called his own living quarters "most wretched" and said they "are all going to pieces; they all leak, and afford but little protection from the weather."

Fort Macon could not have been too unhealthy, for there apparently were not enough sick soldiers to make Coues linger at its hospital. In fact, he commandeered his hospital steward, A. C. Beals, and the two spent endless hours rambling across Bogue Banks. Coues recorded every living thing he saw, from alligators to mud snails, sea urchins to gray foxes. Armed with a shovel, a seine, and a shotgun, he collected thousands of specimens of birds, fish, mammals, reptiles, insects, and marine invertebrates.

On arriving at Fort Macon, Coues asked Baird to send mustard-seed shot, powder, and caps for shooting birds and arsenic for preserving them.

"If so," Coues wrote, "I will give S.I. [Smithsonian Institution] pretty much everything I collect." A shotgun, not binoculars, was the essential tool for a nineteenth-century ornithologist. Coues typically shot fifty to a hundred of each species unless it was rare.

The Annual Report of the Smithsonian Institution in 1869 indicated that Coues donated "two boxes bird skins and osteological collections." He sent other Bogue Banks specimens across the United States, including crustaceans to the Chicago Academy of Sciences and insects to the Boston Society of Natural History.

Coues was not the first naturalist to attract national attention to the Fort Macon–Beaufort vicinity. To my knowledge, that honor fell to William Stimpson, a Smithsonian naturalist who published his "Trip to Beaufort, N.C.," in the *American Journal*

In 1869, Elliott Coues wrote this opening to a study of least terns and Wilson's plovers that he undertook at Bogue Banks.

Mile after mile of sloping sea-beach occupies the front of a low island on the Carolina coast, and contends, along a foamy line, against waves that ceaselessly advance, to be continually repulsed; a sea-front flanked with sand-works blown by the wind into tumuli over the trenches, where lie buried countless shells that will only come to light again as fossils, when the books of today and those who wrote them, have become indistinguishable dust; beyond which there is a vast bed of oozy mire hidden by the rank growth of reeds that rustle and surge with every breath of wind. Among the sand-mounds, defended by these buttresses alike from the open violence of the sea and the insidious approach of the marsh, are sequestered spots, bestrewn with shells, carpeted with slender grasses whose nodding spears trace curious circles in the sand about their roots, with here and there a half-buried vertebra of a stranded whale, or the rib of some ill-fated vessel, telling a tale of disaster by sea,—spots so secluded that the . . . cadence of the wave-beats, conferred by this and that avenue of approach, only enters with an inarticulate murmur. Here is the chosen home of two beautiful birds that come and pass the summer months together.

From Elliott Coues,
"Sea-Side Homes and What Lived in Them,"
American Naturalist (September 1869)

of *Sciences and Arts* in 1860. But much more so than Stimpson, Coues drew the scientific community to Fort Macon. His articles, the collections that he shared so widely, and his habit of inviting his colleagues to visit him at Fort Macon put the Beaufort area on the map for naturalists across the United States.

Other naturalists followed Coues to Beaufort, to Bogue Banks, and to the other barrier islands of Carteret County in the 1870s. News of the region's potential for marine research spread until Johns Hopkins University established a summer laboratory in Beaufort in 1880, the first of several marine research centers located there.

Coues wrote extensively at Fort Macon. He described the nesting habits of least terns and Wilson's plovers in *The American Naturalist*, the anatomy of bird wings for a journal published by the American Association for the Advancement of Science, and the habits of marsh rabbits for a journal published by the Boston Society of Natural History. He probably also did much of his research for a later treatise, "On the Classification of Water Birds," while he was stationed at Bogue Banks.

Not all of Coues's writing at Fort Macon was about natural history. In the surgeon general's 1870 report on United States military posts, Coues made a few observations about the local

Upper left—Derby Flycatcher.

Lower left—Ruffed Grouse.

Lower center—Helmet Quail.

Upper right—Marsh Hawk.

Lower right—Cardinal Grosbeak.

DRAWINGS BY ELLIOTT COUES
From Key to North American Birds, *2nd Edition*

53

Elliott Coues: A Naturalist at Fort Macon

civilians on the mainland, including what he noticed about their eating habits. Shrimp "are scarcely eaten," Coues wrote, but "the oyster . . . is abundant, cheap, and of excellent quality." He observed that yaupon, one of the most common barrier-island shrubs, "furnishes a drink often used by the lower classes as a substitute for tea" and that "venison is sometimes as cheap as beef." He himself seems to have tasted dozens of different species of water birds, shorebirds, and seabirds, excepting only "the most abundant water fowl, the fishing duck (*Merjus serrator*), [which is] hardly eatable."

Coues's greatest accomplishment at Fort Macon was his survey of local animal life. Titled "Notes on the Natural History of Fort Macon, N.C. and Vicinity," the survey was published in five parts (the last two cowritten with H. C. Yarrow, his successor at Fort Macon) in the *Proceedings of the Academy of Natural Sciences of Philadelphia*. The series cataloged in exacting detail local reptiles, fish, mammals, more than two hundred bird species, and marine invertebrates ranging from jellyfish to annelid worms.

Coues's articles comprise a unique catalog of the fauna of Bogue Banks, and they give us a rare benchmark from which to assess ecological changes in the 130 years since he served at Fort Macon. In 1869–70, only a few families inhabited the narrow, twenty-six-mile-long island, so that Coues was describing a coastal world scarcely touched by commercial fishing, much less by the unrestrained tourism and real-estate development of today. Not surprisingly, his "Natural History" refers to a landscape much different from what exists at Bogue Banks now. Not a single home stood by the island's broad ocean beaches in that day, and some of the state's largest maritime forests lined the shore along Bogue Sound. That has all changed. And many animals described by Coues, such as lynx and mink, have vanished due to habitat loss. Whaling was still a part of island life when Coues was at Fort Macon. "The remains of whales," he wrote, were "strawn abundantly along the beach."

Whenever I read Coues's series on Bogue Banks, I am astounded at his passionate curiosity about the natural world and his knack for observing its smallest details. Take his observations on ordinary fiddler crabs (genus *Uca*), the little beasties we see scurrying over every mud flat and salt marsh. Coues, a bird man, did not know any more about fiddler crabs and other crustaceans than you or I when he arrived at Fort Macon. He had never studied them, and he had almost certainly never read a scientific paper devoted to them. Yet merely by looking with care and patience, Coues was able to craft a splendid portrait

ELLIOTT COUES NATURE TRAIL AT FORT MACON STATE PARK
Photograph by Scott Taylor

of the tiny crabs. He described their anatomy, their surroundings, what bird species ate them, what soils they lived in, and how they moved. He charted how deep, at what angle, and at what time of day they dug their holes. He speculated—rightly, it turned out—on their niche in salt-marsh ecology. He even compared the dexterity with which they entered their holes left side first and right side first. (He determined that "the animals went in either side first with equal facility.") And fiddler crabs were only one of the thousands of species that Coues observed while he lived at Bogue Banks.

When I visit Fort Macon State Park today, I usually hike the Elliott Coues Nature Trail, which begins near the fort's main entrance. The little trail winds through a small maritime forest and skirts Beaufort Inlet. When I am there, I think of the trail as more than a memorial to the great ornithologist and his brilliant snapshot of barrier-island ecology a century ago. It is also a good reminder that all of us have the ability to discover nature's wonders, if only we will look.

Elliott Coues: A Naturalist at Fort Macon

THE SCHOONER *ALPHONSO* DOCKED IN BEAUFORT, NORTH CAROLINA, CIRCA 1900
NO PHOTOGRAPHS OF THE *OGEECHEE* ARE KNOWN TO HAVE SURVIVED, BUT THE OLDER *OGEECHEE*
WAS PROBABLY QUITE SIMILAR TO THE *ALPHONSO* AND THE FREIGHTING SCHOONERS THAT PLIED
NORTH CAROLINA WATERS AT THE END OF THE NINETEENTH CENTURY.
North Carolina Maritime Museum Collection

THE SCHOONER
OGEECHEE AT
HATTERAS ISLAND

On a summer morning in 1873, a young man named Cecil Buckman set sail from Beaufort aboard the schooner *Ogeechee*. Bound for Baltimore, he would encounter all the trials of travel at sea—delays and detours caused by shifting winds and storms, currents and tides. Time and again, he nearly lost his life. But through it all, Buckman scrawled a remarkable journal of his voyage and of an unforeseen sojourn at Hatteras Island.

Preserved in a cluttered pantry at the Beaufort Historical Association, Buckman's travel journal provides a fascinating glimpse of sea travel and Outer Banks life a century ago. More than that, though, it offers insight into a hidden dimension of the coastal past, one to which our modern conventions often blind us. I am talking about the different ways that we understand the nature of time—today and in the past, in our world and the sea's.

Buckman's tale of time and the sea begins at the Beaufort waterfront on June 23, 1873. That dawn, the *Ogeechee* sailed for Baltimore. Along with her load of cotton and rosin, she carried the nineteen-year-old son of a local carpenter off to seek his fortune.

At the helm was Captain Sabiston, from one of Beaufort's oldest seafaring families. He was one of several local mariners who commanded "coasting vessels," the schooners and sloops that traded up and down the eastern seaboard and in the West Indies. Though a freighter, the *Ogeechee* was popular among Beaufort residents who preferred to travel with a local master and crew. Sabiston usually proved willing to find them a berth or two.

The *Ogeechee's* voyage started slowly. Becalmed off Cape Lookout, the schooner drifted all day and night, her sails jibing back and forth in the ocean swells. On the second day of the voyage, June 24, a light but steady breeze finally filled the sails, carrying the *Ogeechee* past Cape Hatteras around five-thirty in the afternoon. Sabiston steered her toward Cape Henry, north by east.

Then, near midnight, a fierce storm ripped into the *Ogeechee*. The gale hit when the schooner lay twelve miles east of the northern tip of Bodie Island. All hands rushed to duty stations. To spill the wind, they desperately lowered the gaff topsail, staysail, and flying jib and double-reefed the mainsail. Waves crashed across the deck, and Buckman listened warily to "the mournful sound of the wind whirling through the rigging."

The storm raged all night, until Sabiston had to come about and sail "almost under 'bare poles'" for safe harbor at Hatteras Inlet. "High upon the billows would we rise scanning in our vision the heavens on all sides," wrote Buckman, "then down deep in the trough of the sea leaving only to our view the sides of the mountain waves."

Being forced to seek haven at Hatteras Inlet was a seaman's worst nightmare. Nearing the dreaded inlet the next morning, Buckman saw the skeletons of wrecked ships along the shoals and

bar. But Sabiston had little choice. At midday, he successfully navigated the *Ogeechee* between the dangerous shoals. "Knowing not whether we would pass over safely or strike and be dashed in pieces upon the shore," Buckman stated, "all seemed to be silence." That afternoon, a Hatteras pilot guided the *Ogeechee* on a no less harrowing passage over the bar and into the sanctuary of Pamlico Sound.

Buckman awoke on the twenty-sixth to a clear sky, but the weather still did not favor the *Ogeechee*. A steady northeasterly breeze and heavy swells left by the storm hindered her from sailing back through Hatteras Inlet. The schooner's passengers and crew would have to wait for the wind to shift.

For two days, the passengers of the *Ogeechee* whiled away the hours by the deserted shores of Hatteras Island. They raked clams on the mud flats. They explored old shipwrecks and fish camps. They watched wild horses. Buckman and a fellow traveler raced ghost crabs up and down the beach. And at night, according to Buckman, "all gathered on deck . . . to tell jokes . . . and enjoy the stories of the past."

The crewmen of the *Ogeechee* were accustomed to the sea's temperament. They dried their clothes, whittled, and fished. They dug a well on the shore and filled kegs with water. Every vessel's master saved a variety of chores for just such occasions. Sabiston had his crew scrape down the booms. "For the sake of something to do," Buckman

THE SCHOONER *IOWA*, CIRCA 1900
SWIFT, HANDY, AND OF SHALLOW DRAFT, SCHOONERS SUCH AS THE *OGEECHEE* AND THE *IOWA*
WERE LONG THE MAINSTAY OF COASTAL TRADE IN NORTH CAROLINA.
North Carolina Maritime Museum Collection

noted, "all hands, passengers too, went to work at it."

Sunbaked and sea-salt sticky, the *Ogeechee*'s passengers and sailors would miss or be late for who knows what crucial business deals and family reunions. Who knows, even, what family and lovers might have feared them dead, wondering whether the *Ogeechee*, like so many other vessels before her, had wrecked on Diamond Shoals?

Today, we would scream in frustration. We would pout and fume and protest. We would decry fate and rickety old ships. We would certainly demand our money back, and some would file suit.

But not a note of frustration can be detected in Buckman's journal. If a word of complaint was uttered aboard the *Ogeechee*, Buckman did not see fit to record it.

Time for the *Ogeechee*'s passengers was put on hold. At least for a few days, they fell sway to the sea's own rhythm, a beat not measured by timepiece or datebook but by sun and wind, tides and currents. "Time not our time" is the way T. S. Eliot described the ocean's cadence in his "Four Quartets."

The *Ogeechee*'s quiet interlude at Hatteras Island holds an important lesson about the coastal

The Schooner Ogeechee *at Hatteras Island*

past. We live in a fast-paced and busy world. Airplanes carry us in a couple of hours the distance a schooner sailed in ten days. Computers, telephones, and satellites allow us to communicate instantly across the world. Time clocks govern daily life.

Not so in Buckman's day. A passenger aboard the *Ogeechee* expected delays. A couple of nights stranded at Hatteras Island meant nothing. One could wait far longer for a favorable wind, a willing pilot, or a new spar. Intimidated by shallow, shifting Carolina inlets, many captains waited days just for a fuller moon and a swelling tide. Seagoing vessels might bide storms for a week in port. And a ship caught at sea by a nor'easter might limp into Wilmington or Elizabeth City for bulkhead repairs that stranded her passengers for a month.

The historical record makes the voyage of the *Ogeechee* seem almost swift. I have an account of an 1867 trip merely from Beaufort to Portsmouth Island that lasted five days. And when the Federal armada invaded the Carolina coast early in the Civil War, Union steamers tried to navigate Hatteras Inlet for a month. The fleet nearly withdrew for lack of food and water.

"A Living Gale"

Nothing could be seen except now and then the light of a vessel as it would pass, and the light of the cape now fading in the far distance behind us. The "Old *Ogeechee*" now passing rapidly on with increasing rapidity, and apparently without anything to molest, and having worried through the heat of the past day, all retired except the watch, leaving the guidance in their hands under the care of the overruling Watch above, who so often kindly protects the mariner at sea. Although pleasantly and swiftly we were making our way for Cape Henry when the shades of night overtook us, and we had calmly retired for the night, yet lo! About midnight the dreaded "squalls" were threatening their terror in all directions. The watch having now more than they could manage called others on deck to their assistance for the sails had to be "taken in" or be blown in pieces by the approaching gale. Not demanding the assistance of all "from below," the writer while lying listening in expectation to soon hear the shout of "All Hands On Deck," could but think of the hardships of the sailor, and especially so, while hearing the commands so frequent on such occasions sounding above the noise of the storm, "Take down the Gaff Topsail," "lower the Flying Jib [and] take down your Staysail" and "'reef' the mainsail": then the crashing of the waves washing almost the decks from end to end, the mournful sound of the wind whistling through the rigging, and the screaking and cracking of the spars bending to the strength of the gale.

Having been steering North East three quarters East, at this time we are . . . [coming in sight of the] Coast of [Bodie] Island. The sails all having been put under "double reef," we "laid to" till morning; thinking that then the weather would be more favourable; but Lo! At morning dawn

"Storm off Cape Hatteras, North Carolina," *Illustrated News*, April 23, 1853
North Carolina Collection, University of North Carolina Library at Chapel Hill

"Squalls" were still threatening[.] A North east gale had already begun its rage; almost daring old Neptune to ride its foaming waves, when at twenty minutes to five o'clock, the capt. thinking it more safe not to venture any further, turned and in an opposite direction sailed almost under "bare poles" for Cape Hatteras to make an harbor in H. [Hatteras] Inlet.

Being now about fifty miles distant and fifty miles nearer our destination than the day before very reluctantly was the course taken. "A stitch in time saves nine." Had we continued pressing on against the gale, doubtless serious would [have] been the result: but now with unretarded rapidity did we plow the deep, the wind bearing down upon us with almost a "living gale." High upon the billows would we rise scanning in our vision the heavens on all sides; then down deep in the trough of the sea leaving only to our view the sides of the mountain waves. At eight and a half o'clock the L. [Light] House began to appear in the distance. At 10 having sailed so rapidly, above the noise of the whistling rigging could now be heard the roar of the Breakers on Hatteras Shoals. As we approached, higher would we ascend upon the billows and more daring would the venture appear in crossing: but dangerous or not, having at twelve reached the disastrous part, nothing could be done but to press on. Knowing not whether we would pass over safely or strike and be dashed in pieces upon the shore, all seemed to be silence. All seemed to look at each other without a word of utterance in viewing the dangerous results to which we were so liable to become victims.

From Cecil Buckman,
"Our Trip from Beaufort, N.C., to Baltimore, Md., on Schooner *Ogeechee*" (1873)
Original at the Beaufort Historical Association, Beaufort, North Carolina.

Not only travel, but all of coastal life moved to the sea's measure in the *Ogeechee*'s day. Long before weather radios, fishermen had to read the skies for days before risking the open sea. Clammers and oystermen planned every day around the tide and wind. Up coastal rivers, Carolinians waited months for spring freshets to raise water levels enough for barges and rafts to carry cotton bales and turpentine barrels to port. And many a sailor's wife had to wait uncertainly for a husband's return, for few letters reached home before the mariner himself. An old legend in Beaufort has it that when one of Sabiston's kinsmen, also a mariner, perished at sea, he visited his widow as an apparition to let her know that he had been lost. Alas, not every wife or mother had her fears confirmed so quickly.

Buckman's voyage itself could have lasted far longer. When the *Ogeechee* finally passed back through Hatteras Inlet, she was soon in trouble again. Becalmed halfway across Diamond Shoals, the schooner drifted helplessly toward the beach, until Sabiston had to order the crew to take up oars and row away from the breakers' edge. If the *Ogeechee* had wrecked, the survivors could have waited weeks for passage home. And young Buckman could easily have lost his life. Instead, the *Ogeechee* did at last reach Baltimore, and Buckman went on to make a small fortune in the fruit-shipping business.

The world has changed a great deal since 1873, and our sense of time has changed profoundly since Cecil Buckman's voyage aboard the *Ogeechee*. Tides, currents, and winds are no longer the measure of our days. Nor is our grander sense of time—the sum of our days on this earth—framed by confronting our mortality at every inlet and shoal.

Yet I still wonder whether, down deep, the sea's time has lost its hold on us entirely. Life originated in ocean waters, and there still swells within us a deep affinity with the sea. I am convinced, in fact, that this is an important reason why so many people make pilgrimages to our coast. Maybe it is even why some commercial fishermen are so reluctant to trade a trawler for a time clock, despite the dangers and low pay of their trade. I suspect that, on some level, we all would like to flee the soul-crippling pace of the modern age. We yearn for a moment's renewal, quite literally, in another time.

THE LAST DAUGHTER OF DAVIS RIDGE

W hen I pass the old clam house between Smyrna and Williston, I always glance east across Jarrett Bay to Davis Ridge. You have been that way if you have ever driven Highway 70 to catch the Ocracoke ferry at Cedar Island. Few passersby know that this secluded hammock was once the site of an extraordinary fishing community founded by liberated slaves. Nobody has lived at "the Ridge" since 1933, yet legends of those black fishermen, whalers, and boatbuilders still echo through this Downeast section of Carteret County.

I searched long and hard for the history of those black Downeasterners, and I came to believe that all trace of them had vanished. I found no mention of Davis Ridge in history books. Exploring Davis Ridge by boat and on foot, I lo-cated only an old cemetery, standing silent amid live oaks and salt marsh. All the tattered documents in North Carolina's libraries and archives yielded only tantalizing clues. Then, as I was about to give up, I discovered a tape-recorded interview with Nannie Davis Ward at the North Carolina Maritime Museum in Beaufort.

When interviewed by folklorists Michael and Debbie Luster in 1988, Ward was the last living soul to have grown up at Davis Ridge. A retired seamstress and cook, she was born at Davis Ridge in 1911. She spoke with the Lusters as part of the North Carolina Coastal Folklife Project, whose folklorists tape-recorded the recollections of dozens of Carteret County's oldest residents. Though blind by then, Ward had a strong memory and a

NANNIE DAVIS WARD
Photograph by Debbie Luster / North Carolina Maritime Museum Collection

firm, eloquent voice that left me with an unforgettable vision of her childhood home.

Davis Ridge was an all-black community on a small island near the eastern shore of Jarrett Bay, not far from Core Sound and Cape Lookout. A great salt marsh separated Davis Ridge from "Davis Shore," the mainland to the north. Davis Island was just to the south. A hurricane later cut a channel between the two, but you could walk from Davis Ridge to Davis Island in Ward's grandparents' day.

According to Ward, the founders of Davis Ridge were African American watermen at Core Sound before the Civil War. Some of them were free blacks. Others labored in bondage as pilots, sailors, fishermen, and stevedores. The 1860 census, in fact, listed 117 slaves just at Portsmouth, the northern tip of Core Banks. Many descended from black mariners who sailed to the Outer Banks from the English, French, Spanish, Dutch, and Danish colonies in the Caribbean.

It was Sutton Davis, Ward's paternal grandfather, who settled Davis Ridge. After learning the boatbuilding trade at a Wilmington shipyard, he became a master boatbuilder and carpenter at Davis Island.

When Union troops captured Beaufort and New Bern in 1862, Sutton Davis led the Davis Island slaves to freedom. They rowed a small boat across Jarrett Bay to the fishing village of Smyrna, then fled to Union-held territory. Some of the former slaves founded the North River community near Beaufort, but Sutton Davis bought 4 acres at Davis Ridge in 1865. He and his children eventually acquired 220 more acres there.

The number of black Downeasterners declined sharply after the Civil War, but Davis Ridge remained a stronghold of the African American maritime culture that had thrived along Core Sound. Nearly all of Nannie Davis Ward's relatives worked on the water. Her grandfather Sutton, of course, was a fisherman and boatbuilder. Her mother's father, Samuel Windsor, was a legendary fisherman and whaler born at Shackleford Banks, a barrier island south of Beaufort. (Sam Windsor's Lump is still a Shackleford landmark.) Her father, Elijah, owned a fish house. Her great-uncle Palmer was a seafarer and sharpie captain. Many other kinsmen became stalwarts in the Beaufort menhaden fleet. Among them were the industry's first black captains.

The black families at Davis Ridge were what local historian Norman Gillikin of Smyrna calls "saltwater farmers"—old-time Downeasterners who lived by both fishing and farming. They hawked oysters across Jarrett Bay and raised hogs, sheep, and cattle. They grew corn for the animals and sweet "roasting ears" for themselves. At night, they spun homegrown cotton into cloth. Their gardens were full of collard greens and, as Ward recalled vividly, "sweet potatoes as big as your head." They worked hard and prospered.

Sutton Davis and his thirteen children also operated one of the first successful menhaden factories in North Carolina. He built two fishing boats, the *Mary E. Reeves* and the *Shamrock*. His sons worked the boats, while his daughters dried and pressed the menhaden—known locally as "shad" or "pogie"—to sell as fertilizer and oil.

"Men should have been doing it," Ward explained, "but [my father] didn't have them there, so the girls had to fill in for them." In fact, Ward pointed out, at Davis Ridge, "the girls did a lot of farm working. Factory work, too."

Davis Ridge was a proud, independent community. When Nannie Ward was growing up in the teens and twenties, seven families—all kin to Sutton Davis—lived there. They sailed across Jarrett Bay to a Smyrna gristmill to grind their corn and to a Williston grocery to barter fish for coffee and sugar. But mainly, they relied on their own land and labor. They conducted business with their white neighbors at Davis Shore and across Jarrett Bay by barter and by trading chores. "You didn't know what it was to pay bills," Ward reminisced.

While the Davis Ridge men worked at mullet camps on Core Banks and chased menhaden into Virginia waters, the women cared for farms and homes. They gathered tansy, sassafras, and other wild herbs for medicines and seasonings. They collected yaupon leaves in February, chopped them into small pieces, and dried them to make tea. In May, they sheared the sheep. Nannie Ward's grandmother spun and wove the wool. They produced, Ward explained, "everything they used."

Davis Ridge was a remote knoll, but Ward could not remember a day of loneliness or boredom. She told how two Beaufort menhaden men, William Henry Fulcher and John Henry, used to visit and play music on her front porch. "We enjoyed ourselves on the island," Ward said. "There wasn't a whole lot of things to do, but we enjoyed people. We visited each other."

The camaraderie of black and white neighbors around Davis Ridge was still striking to Nannie Ward half a century later. For most black coastal Carolinians, the teens and twenties were years of hardship and fear. White citizens enforced racial segregation at gunpoint. Blacks who tried to climb above "their place" invited harsh reprisals. The Ku Klux Klan marched by the hundreds as nearby as Morehead City, and word went out in several fishing communities—including Knotts Island, Stumpy Point, and Atlantic—that a black man might not live if he lingered after dark.

A MENHADEN SCRAP AND OIL FACTORY, NEAR BEAUFORT, NORTH CAROLINA, UNDATED
THE MENHADEN FACTORY AT DAVIS RIDGE PROBABLY RESEMBLED THIS RATHER UNIMPOSING COMPLEX.
North Carolina Division of Archives and History

Purse seining for menhaden near Beaufort, North Carolina, undated
Following in the footsteps of the black watermen at Davis Ridge, African Americans have always been the mainstay of the menhaden industry in North Carolina.
North Carolina Division of Archives and History

Davis Ridge was somehow different. Black and white families often worked, socialized, and worshiped together. "The people from Williston would come over to our island," Ward said, referring to attendance at school recitals and plays, "and we'd go over to their place." Sutton Davis's home, in particular, was a popular meeting place. Hymn singers of both races visited to enjoy good company and the finest organ around Jarrett Bay.

Ward even recalled a white midwife staying with black families at Davis Ridge when a child was about to be born, a simple act of kindness and duty that turned the racial conventions of the day upside down.

In the 1950s and 1960s, many white ministers across the South lost their jobs for inviting black choirs to sing at church revivals. Yet the Davis Ridge choir sang at revivals at the Missionary Baptist church at Davis Shore two generations before the civil-rights movement. An old legend even tells how, in 1871, black and white worshipers rushed from a prayer meeting and together made a daring rescue of the crew and cargo of a ship, the *Pontiac*, wrecked at Cape Lookout.

I know that I must be careful not to exaggerate the racial harmony around Davis Ridge. Not a crossroads in the American South escaped the ugliness of racial oppression. But Sutton Davis and his descendants had two things that most black Southerners could only dream of: land and a fair chance to make a living. And unlike the rest of the Jim Crow South, the broad waters of Core Sound could not easily be segregated into separate and unequal sections. Self-reliant, in peonage to no one, the African Americans at Davis Ridge joined their white neighbors as rough equals in a common struggle to make a living from the sea.

Ward left Davis Ridge in 1925. She went to Beaufort to attend high school, then moved to South Carolina and New York. While she was gone, the great 1933 hurricane laid waste to the island's homes and fields. Davis Ridge was deserted when she returned in 1951.

"I still loved the island," Ward told the Lusters only a few years before she died in Beaufort. "When you grow up there from a child, you learn how to survive, you learn everything."

I heard a low, wistful sigh and a deep yearning in her voice. "We were surrounded by so many good things that I don't get anymore, that I never did get again." I knew she was not speaking merely of roasted mullet and fresh figs.

She was silent a moment. Then, with a laugh, she exclaimed, "I'd like to be there right now."

NATHANIEL BISHOP AND THE *SANTA THERESA* CROSSING HATTERAS INLET
FROM BISHOP'S *VOYAGE OF THE PAPER CANOE.*
North Carolina Collection, University of North Carolina Library at Chapel Hill

VOYAGE OF THE PAPER CANOE

A few summers ago, my brother and I paddled down the Waccamaw River, following the path of a daring nineteenth-century naturalist named Nathaniel Bishop. In 1874 and 1875, Bishop made an extraordinary voyage along the Atlantic coast. He traveled nine months and twenty-five hundred miles from Quebec to the Gulf of Mexico in a fifty-six-pound canoe built of varnished paper.

Bishop chronicled his remarkable journey in a long-forgotten book called *Voyage of the Paper Canoe*. This highly entertaining account is to me the most intimate, down-to-earth portrait of the North Carolina coast in the years immediately after the Civil War. During his passage, Bishop discovered a remote world of fish camps and sea-faring villages never seen by wayfarers confined to the coast's main roads and shipping channels. Passing along the Outer Banks, Onslow Bay, and the Waccamaw River, he experienced the best hospitality that local fishing and farming families had to offer. He hauled fish nets with local watermen, shared the lodgings of secluded mariners, and took part in three weddings and other community "jollifications."

My brother and I set off along a part of our coast described in *Voyage of the Paper Canoe*, hoping to rediscover this lost classic and to see how much the coast had changed since Bishop's day.

By the sweltering morning when Richard and I began our voyage, I had learned a few things about Bishop's life. Born in Dedham,

Massachusetts, in 1838, he was a restless spirit. By the age of fifteen, the young explorer had already hiked solo from Boston to the White Mountains of New Hampshire, a trek that lasted twenty-one days. Two years later, in 1855, Bishop shipped out of Boston as a sailor, eager to make a name for himself at sea. Apparently less than enamored with shipboard life, he deserted in Buenos Aires and hiked a thousand miles across South America, a journey that he later described in a book called *The Pampas and Andes*.

Bishop began his voyage down the Atlantic coast in Quebec on July 4, 1874. By the time he reached North Carolina on December 8, he had already overcome several calamities, including a capsizing on Delaware Bay. He had also suffered much skepticism about his "paper" canoe. This featherlight sixteen-foot craft, the *Santa Theresa*, was made of moistened paper overlaid on a wooden frame, then waterproofed and varnished. Inspired by the kayaks of Inuit Eskimos, the design was briefly popular for New England racing sculls and other small recreational craft.

Bishop entered North Carolina on the North Landing River and paddled south into Currituck Sound. The *Santa Theresa* glided over dead remnants of the vast oyster beds destroyed a generation earlier when a hurricane closed Currituck Inlet and cut off the sound's source of salt water. Every

few minutes, he heard "the deep booming of guns"—the sound of market gunners and sport hunters shooting great flocks of ducks, geese, and swans.

After a night at Currituck, Bishop paddled south to Nags Head, on Bodie Island, part of the Outer Banks. He dismissed the village, with its tiny fishermen's huts and boarded-up hotel, as a "forlorn place." The next day, he had to drag the *Santa Theresa* for hours across the shoals on the island's sound side. Chilled and exhausted, he found asylum that night at the Bodie Island Lighthouse, which had been constructed two years earlier. The lighthouse keeper, William Hatzel, sat his guest before a roaring fireplace, fed him warm food, and regaled him with good stories while they listened to the soft cackle of the snow geese outside.

Now wary of Outer Banks shoals, Bishop passed north of Chicamacomico—at what is now Rodanthe—spying only the remote village's windmill and "a high, bald sand-beach" that was gradually smothering a maritime forest. He stayed that night with Abraham Hooper's family at a landmark then known as Kitty Midget's Hammock. The old fisherman put his guest before a great hearth, where the timbers of a wrecked ship warmed the cottage. The next day, Bishop joined the Hoopers in hauling nets for bluefish.

THE ABORIGINAL TYPE (KAYAK.)

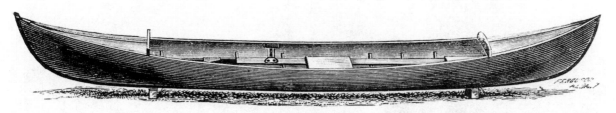

THE IMPROVED TYPE (MARIA THERESA CANOE).

FROM NATHANIEL BISHOP'S *VOYAGE OF THE PAPER CANOE*
North Carolina Collection, University of North Carolina Library at Chapel Hill

At sea again, Bishop accepted a tow from a "cooner" commanded by a Hatteras lad named Lorenzo Burnett. An old-fashioned craft by 1870s standards, a cooner was a long cypress dugout commonly rigged with a mainsail and jib. Although outdated, cooners had certain advantages over plank-built boats. Easily constructed, these seamless boats stood up well to the unavoidable collisions with the shoals of Pamlico Sound.

Arriving at Cape Hatteras, Bishop found a "low range of hills . . . heavily wooded with live-oaks, yellow pines, yaupons, cedars and bayonet-plants." He observed that "the fishermen and wreckers live in rudely constructed houses, sheltered by this thicket." At Hatteras, Bishop strolled beaches crowded with "the gravestones of departed ships."

Then, on Ocracoke Island, he found sanctuary in a shad fisherman's abandoned hut. He had already learned enough from Carolina fishermen to know how to make himself at home. Bishop repaired the hut with sedges and dug a freshwater well in the sand with a clamshell. He slept tranquilly amid wild ponies and wandering sheep.

Bishop soon paddled into Ocracoke village. The local women, he wrote, "can pull a pretty good stroke and frequently assist their husbands with the fisheries." The Ocracokers' impression of Bishop's seafaring was more dubious. Eyeing his paper canoe, one old woman remarked, "I reckon I wouldn't risk my life acrossing a creek in her." A worried oysterman offered to ferry Bishop and his boat across Ocracoke Inlet.

The *Santa Theresa* navigated the inlet safely and cruised by Portsmouth Island. The local cemetery had been rift by storms, and the old seaport's fatal decline had begun. Bishop next sidestepped the shoals at Whalebone Inlet and passed into Core Sound. After paddling sixteen uninhabited miles along Core Banks, he reached the solitary cottage of a schooner captain named James Mason. Mason's family gave him lodging and a hearty supper and treated him "like old friends."

After steering across Core Sound the next day, Bishop arrived at an oystermen's village called Hunting Quarters, known today as Atlantic. "The houses are very small," he wrote, "but the hearts of the poor folks were very large." The villagers lifted his canoe ashore and gave him a bed. The local sailors had just returned home for Christmas. They invited him to three weddings that evening. Fearful of intruding, Bishop was reluctant to join the festivities. But his host, a storekeeper named William Stewart, reassured him. "Invitation!" the storekeeper exclaimed. "Why, no one ever gives out invitations in Hunting Quarters. When there is to be a 'jollification' of any sort, everybody goes to the house without being asked. You see, we are

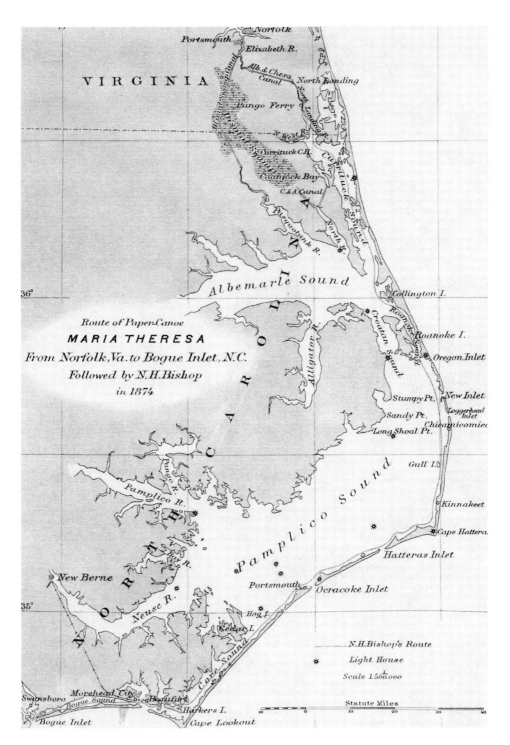

Route of Paper-Canoe

MARIA THERESA

From Norfolk, Va. to Bogue Inlet, N.C.

Followed by N.H.Bishop

in 1874

.... N.H.Bishop's Route

✳ Light House

Scale 1.500.000

Statute Miles

all great neighbors here. Up at Newbern and at Beaufort, and other *great* cities, people have their ways, but here all are friends."

After a night of dancing and revelry, Bishop paddled on to Harkers Island and Morehead City. He spent Christmas in New Bern, then continued south along Onslow Bay.

"The watercourses now became more intricate, growing narrower as I rowed southward," he wrote. "The open waters of the sound were left behind, and I entered a labyrinth of creeks and small sheets of water, which form a network in the marshes between the sandy beach-islands and the mainland all the way to Cape Fear River."

Far more than on the Outer Banks, Bishop observed along the southerly barrier islands the poverty and ruin inherited from the Civil War. All the same, though he stayed at mullet camps, oystermen's cottages, and a peanut farmer's manor house, he never found himself the butt of ill will. Near Rich Inlet, a Confederate veteran named Mosely greeted him by saying, "The war is over . . . and any northern *gentleman* is welcome to what we have left."

Beyond Myrtle Sound, the seacoast no longer offered protection to a small craft like the *Santa Theresa*. Rather than risking the Atlantic, Bishop traveled by cart and railroad forty miles west to Lake Waccamaw, the source of the Waccamaw

River. He ended his journey through North Carolina by descending that "long and crooked river with its dark cypress waters" toward the seacoast of South Carolina.

The Waccamaw in flood season nearly overwhelmed the *Santa Theresa*. "Down the tortuous, black, rolling current went the paper canoe," Bishop wrote, "with a giant forest covering the great swamp and screening me from the light of day. . . . Festoons of gray Spanish moss hung from the weird limbs of monster trees, giving a funeral aspect to the gloomy forest, while the owls hooted as though it were night."

An exhausted Bishop reached the river's first dwelling twenty miles downstream at Old Dock. He continued the next morning "into a landless region of sky, trees, and water." Ten miles later, he came to several small farms as the swampy river bottom gave way to an upland pine forest. He spent the night at Pireway Ferry, then crossed the state line into South Carolina. He reached the Gulf of Mexico on March 26, 1875.

Reading a copy of *Voyage of the Paper Canoe* that I found in the North Carolina Collection, the University of North Carolina's magnificent repository of the state's literary heritage, I was hard-pressed to recognize the Outer Banks of today. The great oyster bays have vanished. Most of the maritime forests have been cleared. Condominiums and hotels now overshadow fish camps.

But when my brother and I joined Bishop's path at the Waccamaw, we found one of America's last great swamp forests. Little seemed different from his 1874 description. The shade of bald cypresses and water oaks darkened the river. Gunmetal gray cottonmouths glided past our boat, and owls crisscrossed aboved us. We paddled beneath a flock of ibises roosting in the treetops, and we gawked at an alligator gnawing leisurely on a deer carcass. We never saw another soul.

Emerging from the swamp at Crusoe Island, I counted my blessings for coastal wild places like the Waccamaw still worth fighting to preserve— and for the spirit of adventure that is renewed in the wilderness.

"A Bright Star in a Dark Night"

The canoe was put into the water on the 16th, and Captain Hatzel's two sons proceeded in advance with a strong boat to break a channelway through the thin ice which had formed in the quiet coves. We were soon out in the sound, where the boys left me, and I rowed out of the southern end of Roanoke and entered upon the wide area of Pamplico Sound. To avoid shoals, it being calm, I kept about three miles from the beach in three feet of water, until beyond Duck Island, when the trees on Roanoke Island slowly sank below the horizon; then gradually drawing in to the beach, the two clumps of trees of north and south Chicamicomico came into view. A life-saving station had recently been erected north of the first grove, and there is another fourteen miles further south. The two Chicamicomico settlements of scattered houses are each nearly a mile in length, and are separated by a high, bald sand-beach of about the same length, which was once heavily wooded; but the wind has blown the sand into the forest and destroyed it. A wind-mill in each village raised its weird arms to the breeze.

Three miles further down is Kitty Midget's Hammock, where a few red cedars and some remains of live-oaks tell of the extensive forest that once covered the beach. Here Captain Abraham Hooper lives, and occupies himself in fishing with nets in the ocean for blue-fish, which are salted down and sent to the inland towns for a market. I had drawn my boat into the sedge to secure a night's shelter, when the old captain on his rounds captured me. The change from a bed in the damp sedge to the inside seat of the largest fireplace I had ever beheld, was indeed a pleasant one. Its inviting front covered almost one side of the room. While the fire flashed up the wide chimney, I sat inside the fireplace with the three children of my host, and enjoyed the genial glow which arose from the fragments of the wreck of a vessel which had pounded herself to death upon the strand near Kitty Midget's

Hammock. How curiously those white-haired children watched the man who had come so far in a paper boat! "Why did not the paper boat soak to pieces?" they asked. Each explanation seemed but to puzzle them the more. . . . We spent the next day fishing with nets in the surf for blue-fish, it being about the last day of their stay in that vicinity. They go south as far as Cape Hatteras, and then disappear in deep water; while the great flocks of gulls, that accompany them to gather the remnants of fish they scatter in their savage meals, rise in the air and fly rapidly away in search of other dainties.

On Thursday I start out for Cape Hatteras. The old sailor's song, that "Hatteras has a blow in store/For those who pass her howling door," has far more truth than poetry in it. Before proceeding far the wind blew a tempest, when a young fisherman in his sailboat bore down upon me, and begged me to come on board. We attempted to tow the canoe astern, but she filled with water, which obliged us to take her on board. As we flew along before the wind, dashing over the shoals with mad-cap temerity, I discovered that my new acquaintance, Burnett, was a most daring as well as reckless sailor. He told me how he had capsized his father's schooner by carrying sail too long. "This 'ere slow way of doing things" he detested. His recital was characteristic of the man.

"You see, sir, we was bound for Newbern up the Neuse River, and as we were well into the sound with all sail set, and travelling along lively, daddy says, 'Lorenzo, I reckon a little yaupon wouldn't hurt me, so I'll go below and start a fire under the kittle.' 'Do as you likes, daddy,' sez I. So down below he goes, and I takes command of the schooner. A big black squally come over Cape Hatteras from the Gulf Stream, and it did look like a screecher. Now, I thought, old woman, I'll make your sides ache; so I pinted her at it, and afore I could luff her up in the wind, the squall kreened her on to her beam-ends. You'd

a laughed to have split yourself, mister, if you could have seen daddy a-crawling out of the companion-way while the water was a-running down stairs like a crick. Says he, ruther hurriedly, 'Sonny, what's up?' 'It isn't what's *up*, daddy; but what's *down*,' sez I; 'it sort o' looks as if we had capsized.' 'Sure 'nuff,' answered dad, as the ballast shifted and the schooner rolled over keel uppermost. We floundered about like porpoises, but managed to get astride her backbone, when dad looked kind of scornfully at me, and burst out with, 'Sonny, do you call yourself a keerful sailor?' 'Keerful enough, dad,' sez I, 'for a *smart* one. It's more credit to a man to *drive* his vessel like a sailor, than to be crawling and bobbing along like a diamond-backed terrapin.' Now, stranger, if you'll believe me, that keerful old father of mine would never let me take the helum again, so I sticks to my aunt at the cape."

I found that the boat in which we were sailing was a dug-out, made from two immense cypress logs. Larger boats than this are made of three logs, and smaller ones are dug out of one.

Burnett told me that frame boats were so easily pounded to pieces on the shoals, that dug-outs were preferred—being very durable. We soon passed the hamlet of North Kinnakeet, then Scarborough with its low houses, then South Kinnakeet with its two wind-mills, and after these arose a sterile, bald beach with Hatteras light-tower piecing the sky, and west of it Hatteras woods and marshes. We approached the low shore and ascended a little creek, where we left our boats, and repaired to the cottage of Burnett's aunt.

After the barren shores I had passed, this little house, imbedded in living green, was like a bright star in a dark night. It was hidden away in a heavy thicket of live-oaks and cedars, and surrounded by yaupons, the bright red berries of which glistened against the light green leaves. An old woman stood in the doorway with a kindly greeting for her "wild boy," rejoicing the while that he had "got back to his old aunty once more."

"Yes, aunty," said my friend Lorenzo, "I am back again like a bad penny, but not empty-handed; for as soon as our season's catch of blue-fish is sold, old aunty will have sixty or seventy dollars."

"He has a good heart, if he is so head-strong," whispered the motherly woman, as she wiped a tear from her eyes, and gazed with pride upon the manly-looking young fellow, and invited us in to tea.

From Nathaniel H. Bishop,
Voyage of the Paper Canoe:
A Geographical Journey of 2500 Miles,
from Quebec to the Gulf of Mexico,
during the Years, 1874–1875
(Edinburgh: David Douglas, 1878)

RICHARD CECELSKI, AMBER-DOG, AND DAVID CECELSKI ON THE BLACK RIVER
Photograph by Scott Taylor

A DAY'S WORK AT A DOLPHIN FISHERY AT HATTERAS ISLAND, 1920S
North Carolina Collection, University of North Carolina Library at Chapel Hill

SMALL MIRACLES

A small miracle happened to me a few summers ago. As I paddled my kayak at The Straits, just west of Brown's Island, six or seven bottle-nosed dolphins suddenly surfaced. They swam so close to my boat that I could have touched them with my paddle. I had watched dolphins from afar all my life, but I was still startled by their size up close, their beauty, and the stallionlike snorts they made as they cleared their blowholes. They stayed at arm's length for a half-hour, rolling alongside me and diving under my boat. If I slowed, they waited. If I sped up, they did, too. In all my years of boating on coastal waters, I had never experienced anything like it.

Too often, I take such small miracles for granted. As a historian, for instance, I tend to view our coastal past as a rather grisly tale of environmental abuses. I forget all we have to be thankful for. Much of our native habitat has been lost, and far too many wildlife species are endangered. But beautiful places and wild things worth fighting for still abound; seashores, swamps, and forests have miraculously survived centuries of settlement, exploitation, and development. It is a miracle that we have them, and that we have a chance to save them for future generations.

The survival of bottle-nosed dolphins is one of those small miracles. Until the 1920s, most coastal residents considered dolphins—or "porpoises," as old-timers still call them—an exploitable resource at best and pests at worst. For more than a century, in fact, they were hunted for their oil and skin. They could easily have been exterminated if conservationists had not convinced our political leaders to protect them by law nearly seventy-five years ago.

Today, we can scarcely imagine the wholesale slaughter of bottle-nosed dolphins that occurred along the North Carolina barrier islands in the nineteenth century. By 1803, slave watermen already ran a dolphin factory near Ocracoke Inlet. Vast numbers of dolphins fed between Bear Inlet and Cape Hatteras every winter, and the enslaved watermen had extra time on their hands because the season's gales slackened ship traffic and lessened the demands for their stevedoring, lightering, and piloting skills. Using small boats, crews of fifteen to eighteen men surrounded the dolphin pods and snared them in heavy, wide-meshed seines approximately eight hundred yards long. Once they trapped them in the surf, the boatmen waded into the water and knifed the dolphins that had not already drowned. Then they gaffed the animals and dragged them ashore. There, they removed their flippers and dorsal fins, stripped and cut the skin and blubber into pieces, and distilled their oil by fire. Each dolphin yielded on average six to eight gallons of oil, which was sold as an illuminant or lubricant.

From that time until the Civil War, only a few dolphin crews operated between Hatteras and Swansboro during the winter. The dolphin industry did not really boom until later. By the 1880s, local fishermen caught thousands of dolphins annually. When a biologist named Frederick W. True visited a dolphin fishery at Hatteras, he found the beach piled high with "skulls and fragmentary skeletons."

In an 1885 edition of the *Bulletin of the United States Fish Commission*, True described both the capture and processing of dolphins. First, the dolphin hunters erected signal poles on the ocean beach a few miles on both sides of their camp. Then they readied from four to six "pilot boats"—sleek, double-ended craft designed to dash through the ocean surf. From these boats, they wielded several eighteen-inch-mesh nets a hundred to two hundred yards long and at least two fine-meshed sweep seines.

When the lookouts signaled that a dolphin pod was approaching, the hunters took to the sea. Circling the pod, they surrounded the dolphins with several nets. "The schools thus entrapped frequently consist of 200 to 300 individuals, the power of which is so great that if they should rush violently against any part of the net it would immediately break," True wrote.

Instead of hauling the nets ashore, the watermen used them to confine the dolphins while their comrades employed sweep seines to capture thirty or forty of the marine mammals at a time. The process took hours. Yet "very few individuals escape, and these mostly by leaping over the nets," True observed.

When True visited the Hatteras fishery, dolphin oil was being sold to merchants in Elizabeth City and Norfolk for $.40 a gallon. One dolphin's oil earned at most $3.20, and an entire season's catch would sell for less than $4,000.00. That sum was divided into shares—one share per man, plus extra shares to the factory owner. By the time the cost of gear, rations, and maybe a tad of apple brandy was subtracted, the take-home pay was slim.

Yet during the heyday of the dolphin industry, Outer Banks families had few other sources of income. Watermen earned a bit of cash as sailors and pilots but made little money in commercial fishing until early in the twentieth century. Although barter and self-sufficiency were still the rules throughout coastal North Carolina, watermen increasingly wanted real dollars for a few luxuries—a new oyster dredge like the ones used by the Chesapeake Bay fishermen, or a bolt of calico or denim that might spare their wives a month of late-night weaving. Hunting dolphins was one of the few ways to afford such labor-saving items.

Oil was the inspiration for dolphin hunting, but it was not the only dolphin product. George Sparks, the manager of a Hatteras dolphin factory, reported in 1885 that the hides made "an excellent article of leather." He also indicated, rather optimistically, that he was experimenting with making sausage from dolphin meat. With his eye on two of the coast's other up-and-coming industries—the menhaden fishery and the guano business—Sparks thought that dolphin carcasses might even make good fertilizer.

The best surviving portrait of a dolphin fishery comes from John W. Rolinson, an Outer Banks man born in 1827. Rolinson lived at Trent Woods (now Frisco) near Cape Hatteras. Like most Bankers, he did a bit of everything to make a living. He was a schoolmaster, a port collector, a seaman, a fisherman—and the superintendent at Colonel Jonathan Wainright's dolphin factory, located halfway between Hatteras and Frisco. For years, Rolinson kept a journal about local happenings, including deaths, shipwrecks, weather, and the number of dolphins slaughtered at Wainright's factory. Wrapped in heavy sailcloth and bound with tough nautical twine, the journal was found some years ago by one of Rolinson's descendants in Elizabeth City.

During the 1886–87 season, Rolinson's crews caught 1,313 dolphins. They had their hands full when they caught 618 in November, but that

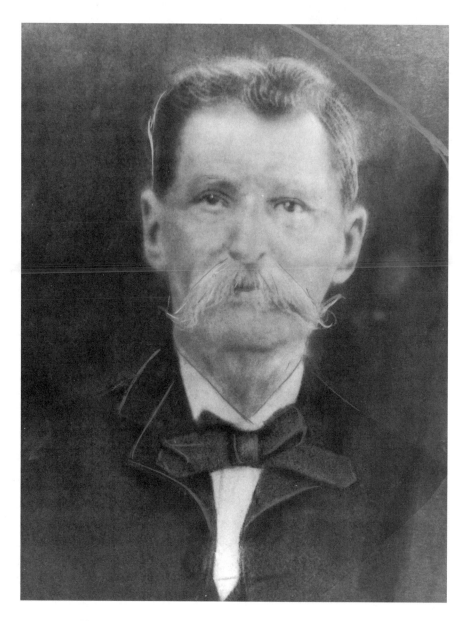

John W. Rolinson, superintendent of a dolphin fishery
at Hatteras Island
Southern Historical Collection, University of North Carolina Library at Chapel Hill

changed dramatically by spring. They put their boats into the surf only six times in March and only twice in May.

One haul could make or break a year. On March 16, 1887, Rolinson's crews captured 136 dolphins in a single day. That was the largest haul in his journal, but editors at the *Weekly Record* in Beaufort had reported a bigger catch the year before at the dolphin fishery at Rice Path, a tiny fishing village on the western end of Bogue Banks. The Rice Path watermen reportedly netted 219 dolphins in a single haul.

The hopes for the dolphin fishery rose and fell frequently during the last decades of the nineteenth century. In the spring of 1887, the *Weekly Record* observed the booming industry with relish. "Over 600 porpoises have been caught this season at Mr. D. Bell's porpoise fishery on Bogue Banks," the newspaper reported that April. The editors boasted that three dolphin fisheries operated in Carteret County that year and that a new factory was being built at Harkers Island.

That same year, a dolphin factory at Hatteras reportedly employed 200 hands and caught 2,874 dolphins. Commercial-fishing boosters dreamed that the dolphin industry might become one of the state's leading fisheries, perhaps on a par with the mullet fishery that stretched from Ocracoke Island to Bear Inlet and the shad fishery centered on the lower Neuse River. The editors of the *Weekly Record* encouraged local fishermen "to at once engage in the catching of Porpoise."

Their vision of dolphin riches proved elusive. The market for dolphin oil fell in the 1890s. Though a dolphin fishery still operated at Hatteras as late as the 1920s, the dream of a multitude of dolphin factories churning out oil, leather, and fertilizer—to say nothing of sausage—never materialized. The peak season seems to have been 1886–87, when four or five factories processed upward of 4,000 dolphins. Overharvesting may have been a factor in the industry's decline. At the Hatteras fishery, the number of captured dolphins fell in the late 1880s, until Rolinson recorded a catch of only 579 during the 1888–89 season.

I would never judge the Outer Banks dolphin hunters by our modern attitude toward these beautiful sea creatures. In the last several decades, marine biologists have discovered that dolphins possess a lively intelligence that makes them seem spiritual kin to human beings. A hundred years ago, dolphins were just another mammal, like deer or cattle. Indeed, many Carolina watermen considered dolphins to be pests because they ate fish that could be caught and consumed by humans. "I believe that in destroying the porpoise we are doing for all engaged in the fishing

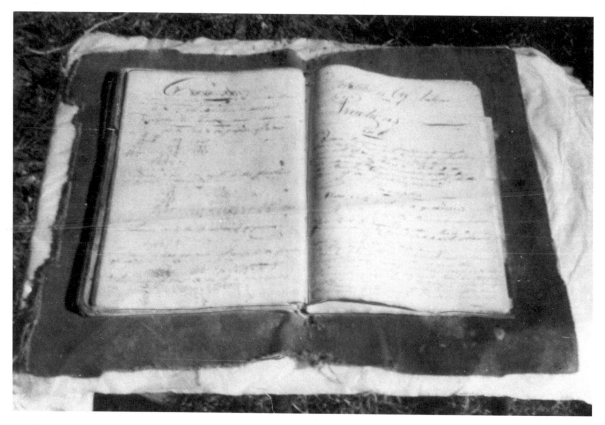

JOHN W. ROLINSON'S JOURNAL OF LIFE AT HATTERAS ISLAND, BOUND IN ITS ORIGINAL SAILCLOTH.
Southern Historical Collection, University of North Carolina Library at Chapel Hill

industry a great service," Sparks wrote in 1885.

I do not think ill of our dolphin hunters of yesteryear, nor do I rue the food and clothing that dolphin oil provided for their families. But I am grateful that conservationists had the foresight to protect marine mammals by law in the 1920s, and that we can still see dolphins in our coastal waters. It is one of the many small miracles that I hope I will never forget.

THE OYSTER SHUCKER'S SONG

I never miss a Mill Creek Oyster Festival. Since 1973, the fire-and-rescue squad at this Newport River community has served up the finest oysters on earth the first Saturday of November. You will find platefuls of fried fish and brimming kettles of clam chowder, but I recommend you head straight to the oyster-shucking shed. If you are lucky, you will taste some of the saltiest, most delectable oysters harvested in America—those taken from the Newport River.

I know, I know. You think your local oysters are better than the Newport River's. I know you folks around Rose Bay, Bay River, and Stumpy Point are mighty proud of your oysters. You Brunswick County old-timers boast of yours, too. And down at New River, you act like you invented the oyster. But even though I know you are all wrong—Newport River oysters are the best—I do not mind people standing up for their home-grown shellfish. I am glad to argue oysters with anybody so long as it involves plenty of shucking and slurping.

There is only one problem: oysters have practically vanished from North Carolina. We are arguing about oysters that we used to have but do not anymore. A century ago, Carolina watermen harvested nearly 2.5 million bushels of the tasty bivalves annually. In recent years, our watermen harvested less than 2 percent of that total, a mere 42,000 bushels. We do not have a single oyster cannery left. Coastal restaurants import oysters from the Gulf of Mexico. And even at the Mill

AN OYSTER SCHOONER AT THE WHARF, WASHINGTON, NORTH CAROLINA, 1884
North Carolina Division of Archives and History

Creek festival, the fire-and-rescue squad has to look beyond the Newport River to feed us hungry hordes of oyster lovers.

What happened to our oysters? The answer is complicated and involves a mix of ecological, economic, and management factors. Without question, though, the turning point in the state's oyster fortunes came in the 1890s. You will never hear a more colorful chapter in coastal history than that of the oyster boom of that decade, but you might also never hear of a period that sounds more like our own.

In 1880, the United States oyster industry was concentrated in Chesapeake Bay. That year, Maryland watermen gathered more than 10 million bushels, a hundred times the amount of oysters harvested in North Carolina. A Norfolk, Virginia, company opened a steam cannery at Ocracoke Island in 1877, but it was hardly typical. Most Carolina watermen tonged oysters just to feed their families. Outer Banks fishermen bartered oysters for corn with mainland farmers every fall, and a few wagoners carted oysters all the way to the Piedmont. But oysters still had so few markets that Pamlico Sound watermen raked up small ones and, not bothering to shuck them, sold them for a few cents a bushel to lime kilns.

The Carolina oyster industry began its ascent in the 1880s. With Chesapeake Bay stocks already diminishing, the Baltimore canneries began to look south. Bair Brothers opened a branch plant in New Bern in 1881, but it was the Moore & Brady oyster cannery at Union Point, also in New Bern, that became the first real success. By 1888, Moore & Brady hired five hundred shuckers at peak season, making it the city's largest employer. Its workers shucked as many as two thousand bushels a day. Virginia canneries also began to send "buy boats" south. They bought oysters from Carolina watermen, then carried them back to Norfolk for shucking, canning, and selling as "Chesapeake Bay oysters."

The potential for the Carolina oyster industry seemed limitless. In 1886, a nautical surveyor named Francis Winslow charted 10,000 acres of oyster beds in state waters. His report on the Newport River estuary was typical. Winslow described "large and thickly stocked beds . . . extending nearly across the river." He counted a whopping 403 acres of oyster beds in the Newport—so many that he found it more practical to sketch where oysters were not than where they were.

The oyster boom hit like a gold rush in the winter of 1889–90. Spurred by new laws opening the state's oyster rocks on an unlimited scale, the Baltimore companies built large canneries in Beaufort, Vandemere, Washington, Belhaven,

Southport, New Bern, and Elizabeth City.

"Men who had never before used an oyster tong could be seen repairing to our oyster banks," W. T. Caho, the state's shellfish commissioner, exclaimed. "All along the marshes . . . could be seen the camps of hundreds and thousands who had never before engaged in the oyster business."

Schooners from Maryland, Virginia, Delaware, and New Jersey stormed the state's oyster beds. As many as fifty Chesapeake boats could be seen in Pamlico Sound at a single glance. They overwhelmed the oyster beds. The newcomers also introduced oyster dredges and longer, sturdier tongs into the local industry. The new gear opened the deepest waters of Pamlico Sound to oystering for the first time.

The boom brought new life to coastal villages. Waterfront streets thronged with local laborers, Chesapeake oystermen, and "Bohemian" oyster shuckers—eastern European immigrants recruited from Baltimore ghettos. According to Kathleen Carter, a historian at High Point University and the leading authority on the oyster boom, Elizabeth City alone boasted at least eleven canneries and seventeen hundred oyster workers in 1890.

"It was a jolly time—a new revelation," reported the *Economist-Falcon*, an Elizabeth City newspaper. "Population and money followed in perpetual stream. New people, new faces, new ways, new man-

ners . . . The song of the oyster shucker was heard in the land." The streets of coastal towns were paved, literally, with oyster shells.

Prosperity bred controversy. Tempers flared between local tongers and Chesapeake dredgers. Reports of oyster poaching, smuggling, and fraudulent leases were widespread. To conserve the rocks, the North Carolina General Assembly prohibited oyster dredging after the 1890 season, but many Chesapeake oystermen refused to heed the law. In 1891, the governor sent the Pasquotank militia, armed with a howitzer, to prevent Chesapeake "pirates" from oyster dredging.

Local oystermen also protested the monopoly held by the Chesapeake Bay companies. They did not want North Carolina oystering to follow in the footsteps of the Chesapeake industry, which was, as shellfish commissioner W. H. Lucas warned in 1893, "in the hands of the large corporations, and the oystermen are nothing more than slaves in the employ of said large syndicates."

The Chesapeake canneries moved south to the Gulf of Mexico when they were finally stopped from oyster dredging. The number of canneries fell to two by 1898. But the oyster boom continued, as sixteen establishments packed raw oysters on ice. Belhaven, Elizabeth City, Oriental, New Bern, Beaufort, Davis Shore, and Morehead City all had packing houses.

The oyster boom depleted the Carolina coast.

This hurt the poor first. A ten-acre leasing system helped prevent big companies from monopolizing the oyster beds, but it took the beds out of the public domain and put them into private hands—usually the hands that had money and political clout. In 1911, Jordan Carawan of Mesic in Pamlico County expressed a common sentiment when he petitioned the general assembly, arguing that the leasing system "deprives poor people of oysters to eat and catch for a living."

The oyster boom also took a heavy toll on oystermen and oyster shuckers. Spurred by the new markets, oystermen worked in frigid winters in small, open skiffs and often spent weeks living in remote, wind-swept camps. "The injury to health from exposure is so great that few ever reach old age," Ernest Ingersoll, a fishery biologist, observed. Oyster shuckers—mainly women and children—had it no easier. Many a coastal young-ster had one ardent hope: to grow up and earn enough money to get Mama out of the oyster house.

By 1909, the boom was over. It had peaked in the winter of 1898–99, when Carolina oystermen harvested 2.45 million bushels. By 1906, state geologist Joseph Pratt was already re-porting a 50 percent decline in oyster harvests. It was the beginning of a long downward spiral for the state's oyster catches. From 1890 to 1908, the industry gathered more than 4 million pounds of shucked meat every year. From 1920 to 1960, a good annual harvest fell to 1.5 million pounds. From 1960 to 1990, 500,000 pounds was a good year. In the winter of 1994–95, our watermen gathered only 228,485 pounds, and our busiest packing houses shucked oysters trucked in from Texas and Louisiana.

Ecological changes since 1960 have made it difficult for oysters to recover from generations of overharvesting. As filter feeders, oysters are notoriously sensitive to water quality, and estua-rine pollutants have risen dramatically in recent decades. Oysters are also highly sensitive to changes in salinity levels. The drainage of coastal wetlands for agribusiness and corporate timber-ing, in particular, has increased freshwater runoff into our estuaries, tainting many of the great oys-ter bays. Land clearing has also heightened the amount of silt flowing into the estuaries, another damper on the health of oyster beds. In addition, since the late 1980s, shellfish diseases have in-vaded coastal waters. While harmless to humans, they have proven catastrophic to oysters.

A century ago, not even the most pessimistic forecaster could have imagined our coast without oysters. Now oystering has almost vanished, and we have nobody to blame but ourselves. I can only pray that we have the good sense to undo what we have done. I am not giving up on the Mill Creek Oyster Festival; I will continue to go and look, hope against hope, for Newport River oysters.

WHERE LATE THE SWEET BIRDS SANG

That time of year thou mayst in me behold
When yellow leaves, or none, or few, do hang
Upon those boughs which shake against the cold,
Bare ruin'd choirs, where late the sweet birds sang.

William Shakespeare, Sonnet 73

When my family visits the beaches at Core Banks or Bear Island, my children delight in watching the sea gulls and sandpipers. The shorebirds enthrall them and, like all children, Vera and Guy revel in a good chase. Watching them among the countless hundreds of birds, I find it nearly impossible to imagine the ocean beaches without those great flocks. That would not have been the case a century ago. Back then, we could have scanned the same wide shores and the sea around them without spying a single tern or gull, and we would have been lucky to see a blue heron or snowy egret among the salt marshes.

T. Gilbert Pearson, a young naturalist from Guilford College, documented the demise of coastal birds at the turn of the twentieth century. One scene from his 1937 autobiography, *Adventures in Bird Protection*, stands out most vividly in my mind. Exploring the barrier islands near Beaufort in 1898, Pearson stumbled on market hunters destroying a seabird rookery. The sight nearly turned his stomach. "For hours," he wrote, the seabirds were "driven up and down the beach and the roar of guns was almost continuous." By the time the shooting subsided, the huge nesting site had disappeared in a cloud of sand, blood, and feathers.

Pearson had not witnessed a rare sight. Between 1880 and 1900, the slaughter of coastal birds was commonplace and relentless. To supply plumage for ladies' hats, market gunners ravaged some of the most common marsh birds, shorebirds, and seabirds in North Carolina. Egrets, herons, willets, cormorants, ibises, shearwaters, and piping plovers all teetered on the brink of extermination. Least terns, laughing gulls, and snowy egrets—visible today by every pier and marsh—had vanished altogether.

Sixty years before Rachel Carson penned her famous warning about DDT and American birds, a no less deafening "silent spring" descended over the North Carolina coast. It fell to Pearson, a tough, unassuming Quaker, to lead a citizens' movement to restore the birds' raucous melody to our shoreline.

Hunting coastal birds was an old custom in North Carolina. Long before market gunning, watermen's families savored wild bird dishes ranging from fried tern to stewed blue heron. In fact, few bird species eluded the cook pot. At Salter Path, a fishing village on Bogue Banks, watermen

and their wives captured songbirds for food by casting fishing nets among yaupon and wax myrtle bushes. Harkers Islanders stewed so many waterfowl that they became known, disparagingly, as "looneaters." And children up and down the coast did not think twice about snaring a prothonotary warbler or a snowy egret. They made for good sport and a tasty meal.

There was a feeling of abundance about all coastal bird life. Even raiding a rookery's eggs did not seem wasteful. Wild bird eggs were enormously popular. Every spring, the townspeople of Beaufort traipsed into Town Marsh in search of fresh eggs. The citizens of Wilmington made excursions as far as Caswell Beach to do their "egging." Street vendors might sell a few eggs and birds, but by and large, local people hunted to meet their own needs.

Hunting coastal birds on that limited scale did not seem to irreparably harm their numbers. When Chowan County lawyer William Valentine visited Beaufort in the fall of 1853, he was astounded by the great flocks on Core Sound. In his diary, Valentine wrote that the birds "darkened the waters in thousands upon thousands."

That changed after the Civil War. A new fashion of decorating ladies' hats with bird plumes fueled an international hunt for feathers. The nation's millinery trade employed more than

Camp Bryan, Ellis Lake, Craven County
Camp Bryan hosted sports hunters from across the United States, including
baseball greats Babe Ruth and Christy Mathewson.
North Carolina Division of Archives and History

eighty-two thousand workers, mostly in New York City, and making ladies' hats was big business. The milliners adorned hats with plumes from birds as varied as flamingos and hummingbirds.

Unhindered by conservation laws, Carolinians hunted coastal birds as never before. Many desperately needed the money. At the end of the nineteenth century, a series of agricultural depressions and damaging hurricanes left many tidewater people in dire straits. Thousands of coastal families migrated north and west in search of a decent livelihood and a better future.

Market gunners first sought coastal birds with the most colorful plumage. Then, as fine-feathered terns, egrets, and ibises disappeared, they turned to more drab species. By 1900, Pearson reported that curlews, willets, plovers, yellowlegs, and dowitchers brought the best prices, but buyers also accepted turnstones, sanderlings, sandpipers, and nearly every other beach and marsh bird.

The gunners also found a burgeoning market for bird meat. Carolina watermen had supplied a few salted-down birds to nearby cities such as Raleigh and Norfolk since at least the 1840s. But by packing the birds in ice—ice making was a technology not widely available until after the Civil War—they could now send thousands fresh by the barrelful as far as Philadelphia and New York City. New railroads and steamer lines helped to open up those markets to the state's shorebirds and marsh birds, as well as to duck, geese, swans, wild turkeys, and other game birds.

The damage to coastal bird populations can scarcely be fathomed. Scores can now be seen shadowing any fishing trawler, but in 1898, Pearson could not find one mating pair of laughing gulls. Gone, too, were the least tern and the snowy egret, a graceful marsh bird highly valued by market gunners for the forty to fifty-two elegant plumes growing along its back between the wings.

A single crew of market gunners led by

"The Plume-Bird Business"

The experiences of that spring and summer left a thousand impressions imprinted on my mind. It was during this time that I found the first Louisiana herons recorded for North Carolina, and by much searching found four of their breeding-colonies. At Cape Hatteras I made the first stilt sandpiper record for the State, and at Great Lake, in the wilds of Craven County, discovered a colony of one hundred and fifty-one pairs of cormorants. It was, and still is, the only breeding assemblage of these birds that has been discovered by ornithologists along the Atlantic Coast between Florida and Maine. On North River I found three white ibises which had migrated from the South, and secured one of them for the State Museum. I know of no other record of this bird from the State. At Orton pond in Brunswick County I took a male water turkey with a nest and four eggs, which to-day may be seen mounted in a group in the State Museum in Raleigh. It was thirty-three years before another nest of the water turkey was found in North Carolina, although it is an abundant species farther south.

I waded swamps, labored through marshes, visited islands and traversed the long, hot beaches of the outer banks where I lived with fishermen and the crews of life-saving stations. Many times I lay down in the shade with wet cloths on my forehead to assuage the frightful headaches that unmercifully assailed me.

The three weeks spent in the unusually beautiful woods at Cape Hatteras yielded many items for my note-book. A nest of the bald eagle with its great clumsy young already on the ground beneath their nest; prairie warblers' nests made almost wholly of wool, gathered from twigs against which sheep had rubbed; wood ducks' nests, three in one day; and on the near-by grassy beaches shore-birds in swarms of un-told thousands. Here and at Ocracoke, Morehead City and elsewhere, I talked with men who had long been engaged in shooting birds for the millinery trade. Terns had been shot by the tens of thousands, and their skins shipped to the millinery dealers of New York. The young, of course, had been left to perish on the hot, sandy beaches where they had been hatched.

A fisherman showed me how to bring terns within gunshot range. A number of them at the time were flying about searching for a school of minnows a hundred yards from our skiff. To a short stick he tied a white handkerchief, leaving two corners flowing, and threw it high in the air. As it fell a least tern darted forward and hovered over the floating object.

"See how easy it is to decoy the first one," he said. "Shoot that bird and another will come and you will soon have the whole flock here."

He told me that most of the killing had been done about shell lumps or sand spits where the birds collect to breed. "They don't like to leave their young," he explained. "At such places I have often shot strikers so fast that I had to put my gun overboard to cool the barrels."

During the conversation he made a statement which I had heard from many others along the coast. "There ain't one striker or gull in a hundred to what there used to be. We've got 'em about all cleaned out."

When I ventured to express disapproval of this wholesale killing of birds he was ready with his answer. "Pore folks have as good a right to live as city people. The good Lord put us here and the Good Book says, 'man shall have dominion over all creatures.' They're ourn to use." He voiced the sentiment of the great majority of the people he knew.

At Morehead City I met A. T. Piner, who had been a great plume-hunter. He told me of feather cruises during which he and his helpers had killed and skinned many thousands of terns and gulls, from Virginia to Florida. In relating plume-hunting experiences, he talked with the same simple frankness that he used in telling about catching mackerel between Beaufort Inlet and Cape Lookout. In each case he was farming the sea for its products. To him and his neighbors the killing of birds and the catching of fish were both ordinary avocations of life. Joe Royal was another famous plume-hunter of Morehead City. He showed me entries in a record book to emphasize the great success which he had achieved on some of his trips. He also spoke of the growing scarcity of gulls and terns.

"It's got so it hardly pays a man to hunt them any more," he declared. "We ought to have a law to protect them until they can catch up their numbers again. If something like this ain't done the plume-bird business will sure come to an end."

From T. Gilbert Pearson,
Adventures in Bird Protection
(New York: D. Appleton–Century Company, 1937)

Augustine Piner of Morehead City boasted of killing 24,000 terns between 1881 and 1884. Piner's gunners also shot untold numbers of other coastal birds, including 175 American egrets and 110 snowy egrets at a rookery near Little River in 1882. They helped to finish off the vast rookeries along the beaches of Carteret County, where more than 10,000 seabirds were said to have roosted just on Shackleford Banks.

A growing market trade in coastal bird eggs only worsened a bad situation. For seabirds already threatened by gunning, the ransacking of a nesting colony's eggs could be the last straw. When "eggers" raided Orton Pond, south of Wilmington, in 1898, they finished off one of the state's last four colonies of Louisiana herons.

Waterfowl populations also plummeted. Currituck Sound gunners, in particular, shipped north the plumes and flesh of tens of thousands of ducks, geese, and swans annually. In addition, the gunners led visiting hunters on bacchanalias of wildfowl shooting, during which a sport club might kill five thousand birds in a day. Shooting without bag limits or off-days, they used many hunting methods now illegal, including live decoys, baiting, and night shooting.

Waterfowl, which bred mainly in the far north, proved less vulnerable to market hunting than the birds that nested on the North Carolina coast.

Nevertheless, around 1900, Henry Ansell, a Knotts Islander born in 1832, estimated that market gunners had reduced waterfowl populations on Currituck Sound to a fourth of what they had been in his youth. Canvasbacks and boobies had all but disappeared.

By the 1890s, many coastal people felt that market gunning had gotten out of hand. Poor families missed having the meat on their tables and the feathers to stuff pillows and mattresses. Fishermen longed for the great flocks of seabirds and shorebirds that had once signaled where they could find schools of fish.

Others fretted over life and limb. In the spring of 1890, two or three crews of Carteret gunners visited Calabash's marshes. "The men . . . seem very clever," a local waterman wrote the *Southport Leader*, "but they are playing havoc with the marsh birds. They keep up a constant bang, bang daily. . . . It is really dangerous for a man to go in the creek and stoop down to catch a clam with a white shirt on."

By the turn of the century, Pearson came to believe that all of North Carolina's breeding populations of coastal birds would soon be exterminated. Fortunately, out of this ecological calamity came a hopeful sign of a brighter future for coastal wildlife. In 1902, the plight of coastal birds inspired the founding of the state's

WATERFOWL HUNTERS WITH THEIR TROPHIES ON THE DECK OF *THE PARKINS*
New Bern - Craven County Public Library

first wildlife conservation group, the North Carolina Audubon Society. The society became a model of citizen activism, helping coastal birds toward recovery and also inspiring the state's people to campaign for the protection and wise management of other wildlife.

Pearson was the North Carolina Audubon Society's first secretary. Led by him, the society advocated successfully for restrictions against the killing of water birds and songbirds. In 1903, the general assembly granted the society the authority to employ wardens and enforce the new laws. This made North Carolina the first Southern state to adopt a regulatory system of bird and game protection.

The Audubon wardens met stiff opposition. They risked violent reprisals for arresting offenders. They ran up against a booming black market in illegal game. And local juries proved reluctant to penalize violators of the new conservation laws. Resistance might have been less ardent if the new legislation had prohibited only market gunning, not shooting for local consumption. But the Audubon activists were skeptical of halfway measures. Then in 1906, the Gunners' and Fishermen's League in Currituck County began to organize political opposition to, in a local newspaper's words, "the Honorable T. Gilbert Pearson and his legion of women and children backers."

In 1909, responding to this backlash, the general assembly stripped the Audubon Society's authority over bird and game conservation. By 1916, North Carolina was the only Southern state except for Mississippi without such a regulatory system. Not until the passage of the Enabling Act to the first federal Migratory Treaty in 1918 did conservation enforcement get real teeth. By then, New York had cut off most market gunning by outlawing any trade in plumage across its borders. North Carolina finally created its own bird and game conservation agency, the North Carolina Game Commission, in 1927.

Despite setbacks, the early Audubon activists made important strides. In addition to advocating stricter conservation laws, they purchased key island rookeries as preserves and nourished a growing public interest in wise stewardship of the state's natural heritage. By World War II, most of North Carolina's coastal birds had rebounded. Only piping plovers seem never to have recovered fully from the millinery trade. Ecologists today consider the recovery of the marsh birds, shorebirds, and seabirds of the Atlantic coast one of the great triumphs of modern conservation.

Pearson devoted his life to bird conservation. In 1937, near the end of a long and fruitful career, he reflected on the dark days of the great coastal bird hunts. Pearson hoped lessons had been

MAUD INEZ TILLMAN, JUNIOR SECRETARY, AND THE MEMBERS OF THE JUNIOR AUDUBON SOCIETY OF
ELIZABETH CITY, FROM *AUDUBON SOCIETY OF NORTH CAROLINA ANNUAL REPORT*, 1907
North Carolina Collection, University of North Carolina at Chapel Hill

Punt gun of the kind used by market gunners to shoot ducks and geese, Currituck County, from *Audubon Society of North Carolina Annual Report*, 1907
North Carolina Collection, University of North Carolina at Chapel Hill

learned. He hoped a new era of respect for wild-life had arrived and a new empathy for nature's frailty had been reached.

Pearson remembered, too, a bit ironically, how much he used to enjoy the market gunners' company. Many an evening, he shared a gunner's hearth. He had found them brave, daring men. They brimmed with feistiness, knew the wild, and told raucously good tales. He respected many of them. In his eyes, a lifetime spent in bird conservation cast no ill light on the gunners. It was the system that "encouraged overkilling of the bird supply," Pearson had always argued, "that must be changed."

Sanderton store at Buffalo City
Hubert Ambrose Collection, Outer Banks History Center

In the Great Alligator Swamp

Early one March, I disappeared into the Great Alligator Swamp. After being cooped up all winter, I needed to get into the wild. At the first hint of spring, I drove to the Alligator River National Wildlife Refuge, between Columbia and Manteo, and slipped my boat into an amber-red creek fragrant of peat and sweet bay. Only in ancient peat swamps—the Dismal, the Croatan, the Okefenokee—have I ever smelled earth so uproariously rich in life. I loaded my boat with groceries, gear, and extra clothes and paddled into the swamp, never looking back.

I picked the Great Alligator because it is such a grand wilderness, more than 160,000 acres of remote, uninhabited swamps, hammocks, and lakes. But I also wanted to see what remained of

Buffalo City, an abandoned sawmill village that thrived by Mill Tail Creek in the heart of the swamp between 1885 and 1925. It was once the largest town in Dare County and boasted one of the busiest sawmills in North Carolina.

Dozens of mill towns like Buffalo City sprang up in coastal North Carolina between 1880 and 1920. American timber companies had exhausted the forests of New England and the Great Lakes, so they moved to the South. Soon, they logged our old-growth forests and moved on again. When the last stands of Atlantic white cedar (known locally as juniper) were cut, Buffalo City became a ghost town.

As I paddled into the Great Alligator, I had a guidebook better than all of my topographical maps. My barber and friend, Bud Midgette, who hails from Columbia in nearby Tyrrell County, had recently honored me with a copy of his late uncle's unpublished reminiscences. That uncle, Benjamin Nathan Basnight, worked at Buffalo City in the 1920s and lived all but a few years of his life around the swamp. At different times, he was a logger, farmer, fisherman, boatbuilder, and rum-runner. With his reminiscences—written in 1969 for his granddaughter, Selina Basnight Stokes—in hand, I spent several days in and around the Great Alligator.

Basnight was born in 1895 at Second Creek, a small community of loggers, farmers, and shingle makers in Tyrrell County. He moved with his family to Alligator Creek in 1901. Basnight spent his childhood in the woods hunting, fishing, "bull frogging," and doing, in his words, "a thousand things a boy could do." By the age of twelve, he was helping his daddy in the woods and on their one-mule farm.

At twenty-one years of age, Basnight worked for a commercial fisherman and lived at a fish camp on Charles Island, at the mouth of Alligator Creek. "We did not do too well," he confessed, "but we paid for our nets and eat beans regular and had lots of fun doing it."

After his father died of typhoid fever in 1919 and the cotton market crashed the next year, he gave up farming. Like many other Dare County residents, Basnight had few choices but to find a mill job. In September 1922, as he recorded, "I put out for Buffalo City."

So did I, seventy-five years later. On my first day in the Great Alligator, I paddled down Mill Tail Creek to the old site of Buffalo City. A swamp forest of cypress, pond pine, sweet gum, and maple trees had replaced the village. The only relics that I could find were a few railroad tracks and a beat-up concrete wall, part of the old pulp mill. I had to rely on Basnight's memoir to bring the deserted swamp back to life.

Buffalo City thrived many years before Basnight's arrival. In the 1880s, a New York timber company called Buffalo City Mills located the sawmill village in the swamp about nineteen miles west of Manteo. Local laborers and, according to oral tradition, more than two hundred Ukrainian immigrants from New York raised the town on the northern bank of Mill Tail Creek. In such swampy land, they had to build streets by laying planks and covering them with a thick layer of sawdust.

In 1907, the Dare Lumber Company bought the mill village. The company owned Buffalo City's houses, general store, sawmill, school, churches, and hotels. Local white laborers lived downtown, but blacks and Ukrainians lived together in a

STEAM SKIDDER AND LOGGING CREW OUTSIDE OF BUFFALO CITY
Hubert Ambrose Collection, Outer Banks History Center

neighborhood to the south. Basnight wrote that about three hundred people inhabited Buffalo City. Other workers commuted from outlying settlements such as Sycamore and Sandy Ridge.

The company paid wages in scrip, pieces of brass or aluminum redeemable only at the company store. "You had to buy groceries there, so that came out of your pay," former Buffalo City resident Hubert Ambrose told the *Virginian-Pilot* years ago. "Sometimes, at the end of the week of work, you'd wind up owing them money. The company store really owned you."

Basnight's memoir agrees. "Most of them [made] less than $2.00 a day and traded it out at the company store," he recalled. "A lot of them would never see a dollar, just . . . 000 on their envelope."

Buffalo City was a rough, wild, and raucous place not for the mild of heart. The timber company made the laws, and vigilante justice enforced

"Another Tom Sawyer"

On Jan. 1st 1905 my Father pulled up stakes and moved on a small farm near by.

It was here I started growing up with several boys about my age with a new outlook on life[.] Still Rambling the woods hunting—fishing—bull frogging and a thousand things a boy could do.

Yes, Selina[,] I always had my cat and dog. The dog and I were inseparable when I might be in some canal swimming.

But I did most of my swimming in the [Albemarle] sound. I always went to church on Sunday morning and as soon as I get home and got my dinner I would make a bee line to Rogers Landing.

The last thing my Mother would tell me as I went over the fence was (boy don't you go in swimming)[.]

Yes Mam or no Mam[,] She knew I went but she must have been so glad to see me coming back she would not say anything[.]

I guess I was another tom sawyer[.]

Sometimes about this age I got me some steel traps and in the fall and winter I set them for coon and opossum[.] By trapping and Frogging in the spring I could buy part of my clothes[.] What I could not buy Mother would make[.]

Speaking of catching frogs[—]

Sometimes I would walk down some old ditch where they would be sitting on the bank, and when they jumped in I would watch where the bubbles were coming up, then get in the ditch and make a grab. Not many times that I failed to get my frog.

But once I failed. I come up with a red bellied moccasin around the neck. Well nobody had to tell me when to turn it aloose.

It was about this time that my Father introduced me to the north end of a mule going south.

From the unpublished autobiographical notes of Benjamin Nathan Basnight (1895–1971). Copy in the possession of Mr. Bobby Basnight, Newport News, Virginia.

TRANSFER STATION AT MILL TAIL
Hubert Ambrose Collection, Outer Banks History Center

them. Stories of the village's wooden stocks can still be heard in Dare County. "That was a Saturday afternoon thing, watching people get punished," one fellow remembered. "They'd whip them till the blood ran down their backs. Leave them locked there for up to two days. Make a 250-pound logger cry."

To supply Buffalo City with logs, timber camps arose throughout what are now the wildest parts of the Alligator River National Wildlife Refuge. Even Whipping Creek, where I paddled my second day, once had its own post office. Today, only black bears, white-tailed deer, and recently reintroduced red wolves inhabit that area, but timber workers once built narrow-gauge railroads into the darkest interior of the swamp. Mules hauled the logs to the railroads, and steam locomotives carried them to loading docks at Mill Tail Creek.

Basnight built railroads when he first moved to Buffalo City. He recalled, "My work building railroad was hard but I enjoyed it. It consisted of clearing a 12-foot right of way of trees and putting down the run poles, then cross ties. I could build 15 yards per day and get 20 cents a yard."

He later was a foreman on a skidder, a small, steam-powered railroad engine that dragged logs to the main railroad tracks. He also ran a gas locomotive.

Life at Buffalo City was hard, but also had its pleasures. "With this many people in such a small place, there was never a dull moment, for all the young folks would be gathered somewhere every night," Basnight said. "But bedtime was not later than 10 o'clock. Everybody was up next morning by 4:30 in order to catch the train into the woods at 6 o'clock."

The Red Onion Hotel, where Basnight lived, was the scene of weekly dances featuring well-known Dare County fiddlers such as Webb Ambrose and Jessie Smith. At one of those dances in 1924, "I got my eyes on a young girl in a blue serge sailor suit," Basnight recalled. Soon, he and that girl were taking boat trips down Mill Tail Creek and paddling up to Sawyer Lake to pick water lilies. "Well," Basnight told his granddaughter, Selina, "it was many years later you learned to call her Mama."

Basnight enjoyed the camaraderie of the mill workers and loggers at Buffalo City. "There was only one class of people here," he said. "There was no upper crust. Everybody eat their dinner of beans and sow belly out of a tin bucket and washed it down with black coffee—and worked ten hours a day at 15 cents per hour. . . . They would take you at face value and never question your past."

The last old-growth timber in the Great Alligator was soon cut. The Dare Lumber Company went bankrupt in 1917, and none of its successors lasted very long. Basnight lost his job when the last of the big lumber companies closed in 1926. He stayed a few more years to build a small sawmill for Duvall Brothers and to cut juniper logs near Beechland, farther up Mill Tail Creek.

Buffalo City did not disappear right away. The famous East Lake moonshining business kept the old mill town afloat during Prohibition. But after the liquor trade was made legal again in 1934, the boom town gradually faded into a ghost town. Basnight returned for a while, building a home for his family in a shady grove of sweet gum and cypress trees (with a lawn two feet deep in shingle dust) in 1935. He later made a living as a boatbuilder in Elizabeth City, where he crafted moth boats and flat-bottomed fishing skiffs. He died in 1971.

Buffalo City's survivors and their descendants still gather for an annual homecoming at Mount Zion Methodist Church in East Lake, but nobody lives by Mill Tail Creek today.

I had a wonderful three days in the Great Alligator. I enjoyed the swamp's serenity, and the mosquitoes, ticks, and cottonmouths had not begun stirring yet. I did get drenched near Sawyer Lake—I am not telling *that* story—but I was lucky enough to find an old logging bridge where I could dry out. I was thrilled to explore the Great Alligator and, with Basnight's help, to discover a forgotten world whose memory might otherwise have faded, like Buffalo City, into the swamp.

NAVASSA GUANO COMPANY, CIRCA 1905
New Hanover County Public Library

THE GUANO GOSPEL

The smallest places sometimes have the grandest stories. I thought about this recently when I visited Navassa, a town a few miles outside Wilmington. A rural, mainly African American community, Navassa is surrounded by cypress swamps and rivers. It is a remote, quiet place without even a small downtown—just country homes with gardens, an old graveyard, a lumberyard, a volunteer fire-and-rescue squad, a Masonic lodge, Mount Calvary AME Church, and a couple of abandoned fertilizer factories. You would never guess that Navassa's past spans continents and seas—or that it upends much of what we think about coastal history.

Navassa's story begins with the guano fertilizer boom that swept America in the nineteenth century. Guano, from the Quechua word *huano*, meaning dung, originally referred only to the dried excrement of seabirds. When the German explorer and scientist Baron von Humboldt visited Peru early in the 1800s, he found that some of its rookery islands had hundred-foot-thick layers of bird droppings. Countless generations of albatrosses, gulls, penguins, cormorants, and other seabirds had caked the islands with their nitrogen-rich dung.

Introduced to Europe by Humboldt, Peruvian guano was an extraordinarily rich source of ammonia, phosphate, and other nitrogenous compounds, as well as a source of alkaline salts, sulfate of lime, and other organic matter that improved plant growth. Demand for guano fertilizer soon raged across Europe and America.

Peru nationalized its guano deposits around 1840 and ran the guano business as a state monopoly. For the next forty years, the country earned most of its foreign exchange by selling dried bird feces. During the middle of the nineteenth century, the "guano gospel" spread like wildfire. The use of commercial fertilizers rose especially fast in the American South, where the rate of soil exhaustion was high, competition from Western lands was intense, and agricultural practices were relatively inefficient. By 1854, United States guano imports exceeded 175,000 tons a year, and by 1860, guano represented 43 percent of all commercial fertilizer used in the United States.

To procure cheaper sources of guano, Congress passed the Guano Islands Act in 1855. Under this law, American entrepreneurs could claim any uninhabited island in the world if it had the potential for guano mining. Under the terms of the Guano Islands Act, United States investors eventually claimed ninety-four islands, rocks, and keys, including a tiny limestone crag between Jamaica and Haiti known as Navassa Island.

The guano at Navassa Island was not mainly bird excrement; it was calcium phosphate and limestone that had been produced by the tectonic uplifting of coral reefs. Though not competitive in quality with Peruvian guano, Navassa Island's

guano—as it was still known—was more affordable. This was an especially important consideration after the Civil War, when few Southern farmers could afford the luxury of Peruvian guano.

A group of Wilmington businessmen established the Navassa Guano Company in 1869. The businessmen hoped guano would be a good return cargo for the seagoing vessels that carried lumber and naval stores to the Caribbean. To keep the guano's acrid smell out of Wilmington, they built their factory a couple of miles away on a marshy peninsula at the confluence of the Brunswick and Cape Fear Rivers. Originally, the company imported phosphate rock from Navassa Island. The island soon grew famous for its abundance of guano and infamous for its working conditions, deemed by one observer to be "above all known types of punishment." These conditions led to a notorious uprising by guano miners in 1889 in which at least four overseers were killed.

Navassa Island was not mined after 1898, but the Navassa Guano Company adjusted. *Guano*, which originally referred only to bird droppings, became synonymous with any kind of manure. The Navassa company made fertilizers with nitrate of soda from Peru, potash (wood ash) from Germany, fish from the Atlantic Ocean, phosphate rock and cottonseed from other Southern states, and blood and bone from Midwestern slaughterhouses. By 1912, the company employed about three hundred workers and produced fifty thousand to sixty thousand tons of fertilizer a year. And the fertilizer industry, led by the Navassa Guano Company, became the most important in Wilmington.

Today, Navassa is an incorporated town of about six hundred residents, most of them African Americans whose ancestors worked in the guano industry. In the company's earliest days, "if you worked at the factory, you could live in the former slaves' quarters for free," according to Eulis Willis, a local civic leader who wrote *Navassa: The Town and Its People*. Former slaves from local rice plantations worked at Navassa, and a guano boom town materialized amid the old rice fields and cypress swamps. Fifteen houses, two single-men's quarters, and two stores arose at a site known as Bluff Hill.

The town of Navassa grew up around the Navassa Guano Company. "The factory was the lifeblood of this community," Willis recalled. Toward the end of the nineteenth century, the guano workers began to buy their own land, particularly along a small stream known as Dogwood Neck. The company still possessed much of the local housing, a company store, and its own police force, but the black workers gained a fierce independence by owning land and having regular wages. By the

1920s, Navassa was, in Willis's words, "a booming, wide-open town." It had six social clubs, numerous cook shops where the guano workers could buy a meal, and trains that stopped four times a day on their way in and out of Wilmington. Other fertilizer companies also located in Navassa, employing as many as two thousand workers in their heyday.

I have not found a good description of the inner workings of the guano factories in Navassa, but in 1897, a reporter from the *Wilmington Messenger* toured the nearby Almont Fertilizer Company and described the factory in some detail. Founded in 1882 by Powers, Gibbs and Company, a British firm that had a monopoly over the sale of Peruvian guano in Europe and North America, Almont occupied a bluff on the Northeast Cape Fear River a couple of miles above Wilmington.

As described by the *Messenger*'s reporter, the factory workers first used mills to grind phosphate rock—brought by rail from mines in Florida, South Carolina, and Tennessee—into powder. Then they separated the phosphate from the silica in great vats of sulfuric acid. The dissolved rock phosphate could be mixed with different combinations of potash, salt, blood, dissolved bone, and other ingredients to make a variety of fertilizer brands. Finally, the mixture was dried, lumps were broken up, and it was put into bags.

The Almont Fertilizer Company, like most of the local factories, also produced its own sulfuric acid. Working in the "acid factory" was fraught with danger because of the lethal acid and its fumes. The factory floor must have resembled a scene out of Dante's *Inferno*. The black laborers burned pyrite ore mined in Spain and Newfoundland in two dozen furnaces. "The heat from the fires drives the sulphur from the ore in fumes," the reporter wrote. The fumes condensed into sulfuric acid, which flowed through lead pipes into the fertilizer factory next door.

The Navassa Guano Company and the Almont Fertilizer Company were among more than a dozen fertilizer factories operating in the Wilmington area by 1912. The Pocomoke Guano Company, founded about 1910, located its factory in the remote community of Pocomoke, settled by ex-slaves from a local rice plantation just after the Civil War. Located off U.S. 421 by Carolina Power and Light Company's Sutton Steam Plant, the deserted remains of the Pocomoke community have recently been the subject of research by Mariel Rose, an anthropology student at the University of North Carolina at Wilmington.

One of the local people Rose interviewed about Pocomoke was Hortense Moss, whose mother and grandmother fed guano workers out of their kitchens. "They had all the black people that would come over there to work in fertilizer for five dollars a week," Moss said. "My grandmother was a cook, and she'd sell a cup of coffee for five cents and a meal for fifteen cents."

The bustling village that arose by the guano factory had its own school, a livery stable, a restaurant, about twenty houses, and at least five bunkhouses for unmarried workers. "We would get together, cook and talk and eat and have church in each others' home," Moss's mother told her. The residents of Pocomoke would "go to each others' houses and sing and pray. It stayed that way for years."

Other fertilizer factories depended heavily on the local mining of marl, fossilized seashells rich in calcium that had the much-desired effect of fixing nitrogen in manured soil. The expansive marl deposits found throughout much of the North Carolina coast were first mined commercially just after the Civil War.

G. Z. French's lime and phosphate facility at Rocky Point was perhaps the best known of these marl mines. Like many fertilizer pioneers, French got into the business through his agricultural interests. An innovative farmer with extensive holdings of truck vegetables, he continued to farm while he engaged in the fertilizer trade.

The Mammoth Fertilizer Establishment of the Navassa Guano Company, of Wilmington--Its Interesting History and Development. Pioneer in the South of This Big Industry.

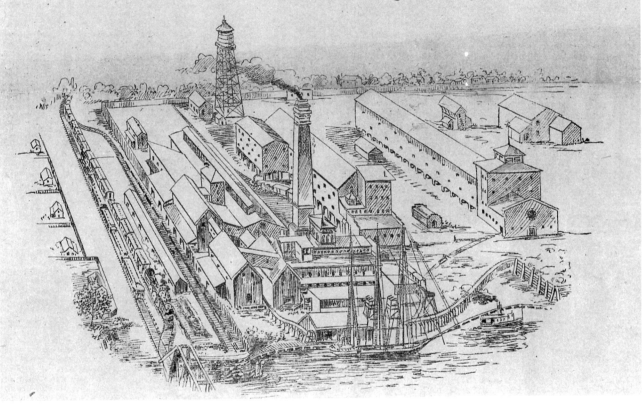

NAVASSA GUANO COMPANY, WILMINGTON, 1897 FROM THE *WILMINGTON MESSENGER*
Bill Reeves Collection, New Hanover County Public Library

A different kind of fertilizer company operated at Cronly, about seventeen miles west of Wilmington. Established in 1883, the Acme Manufacturing Company concentrated on cottonseed oil. According to the *1884 North Carolina Business Dictionary*, the ten-acre factory complex also made fertilizer out of "peanuts, palm kernels, linseed, flax-seed or any other oil-yielding substance which they can obtain" and experimented with oil distilled from longleaf pine needles. Acme never succeeded in making a practical fertilizer out of pine needles, but from roughly 1886 to 1901, the company did sell a variety of pine-needle products, including mats and carpets, upholstery, mattresses, cotton bagging, and a medicinal oil known as Pinoleum.

Even the menhaden fishing industry was an important part of the guano business. According to Barbara Garrity-Blake, author of a fascinating portrait of the menhaden industry called *The Fish Factory*, the name *menhaden* came from the Native American word *munnawhatteaug*, meaning "that which manures." The menhaden factories in Beaufort, Morehead City, and Southport comprised the state's largest fishery in the first half of the twentieth century. They eventually produced mostly fish meal, an important additive to livestock feed. But into the teens and twenties, the menhaden catch was used principally for guano. By 1907, North Carolina had at least ten fish factories that processed approximately 57 million pounds of menhaden, much of it destined for the Navassa Guano Company.

This forgotten tale of the fertilizer industry may not be the most romantic part of our coastal history. We are talking about bird droppings and manure, after all. But that does not mean that we should forget it. Countless souls shoveled guano and phosphate rock in our ports. Many others sweated through twelve-hour shifts in sulfuric acid factories or trudged through the darkest nights to make the first shift at fish factories and marl mines.

These mostly unremembered workers tried to make a decent living and build a better future. They worked hard; a lot of them died young; and I do not expect many of them got a fair shake. But they are as much a part of our coastal past as anybody. Their stories remind us of how many coastal voices have not yet been heard. And lest we forget, they remind us that there is often a big story in even the smallest places.

MIS' BASHI AND THE LADY DOCTOR

Whenever I visit older coastal cemeteries, I am always moved by the small gravestones etched with little lambs and baby angels. Often, I find them clustered together—three, four, or even more children from a single family. And it is not unusual to discover a young mother buried nearby. At Harlowe United Methodist Church, between Beaufort and Havelock, is a typical cluster of graves, all children of Craven and M. T. Taylor: Vernon, age two; Early, nine months; Lila, four months; Nina, twelve days; and Daisy, who was born and died the same day. You can find similar heart-wrenching scenes in nearly every graveyard established before World War II.

These gravestones bear witness to the dangers of childbearing and childhood diseases before the advent of modern obstetrics and vaccines. Even as late as 1910, one mother out of thirty died during childbirth in the United States (com-pared to fewer than one in five thousand today). Every pregnancy forced a woman to contemplate the possibility of her own death even as she readied herself to bring life into the world. And if childbirth was not perilous enough, a host of infectious diseases—from typhoid fever to diphtheria—posed a lethal threat to every mother's child.

We rarely find historical records that illustrate how the "shadow of maternity" shaped coastal women's lives. Childbirth and children were considered women's sphere and, as such, a private affair not really part of history. Even midwives and physicians rarely left written accounts of their experiences delivering babies and caring for young children.

The saga of an Outer Banks midwife named Bathsheba Foster and a woman physician named Blanche Nettleton Epler is a rare exception. They were an unlikely pair: an illiterate, self-taught midwife who had delivered babies for forty-five years and a worldly Midwestern doctor who was one of the first women to graduate from the Johns Hopkins School of Medicine and the first woman appointed to the United States Coast Guard. Their story, which unfolded in an article Epler wrote for *National Geographic* in 1933, offers at least a glimpse of the shadow of maternity and the women healers who struggled to dispel it.

Epler had cared for women and children many years before she met "Mis' Bashi" at Hatteras Island in 1923. Nearly sixty years old then, Epler had grown up in an upper-class family in the small town of Jacksonville, Illinois. She was one of only two women in the Johns Hopkins class of 1899. (Johns Hopkins was the first mainstream medical school in the United States to admit women, a policy stipulated by a group of women patrons who donated half a million dollars to found the medical school in 1893.) She interned at the New York Infirmary for Women and Children, then was a general practitioner, a college teacher, and a public-health pioneer in Kalamazoo, Michigan, from 1901 to 1923.

I do not know why Epler left Kalamazoo to accept a United States Public Health Service post at the Coast Guard station at Hatteras. She never married or had children, and she gave up many personal comforts and access to the latest medical technology to come to the Outer Banks. More-

over, she had built a successful career in Kalamazoo. She had co-founded a Methodist hospital, two nursing homes, and the local Girl Scouts chapter and had served as the city's bacteriologist.

Certainly, Epler had an adventurous spirit. Women physicians of that day tended to be daring, or they would never have broken into medicine in the first place. At the same time, Epler had a deep commitment to public health that may have inspired her to serve at Hatteras. She seems to have found the Outer Banks an exciting opportunity to prevent needless deaths from childbearing and from infectious diseases such as tuberculosis that had proven treatable with improved public-health practices. She had earlier been involved in public-health campaigns in Michigan and in the hookworm crusade in the South.

Beyond her spirit of adventure and her commitment to public health, Epler also may have left Kalamazoo to find a more meaningful way to pursue her calling at a time when the status of women physicians was declining. The women among United States physicians had peaked at about 6 percent in 1900, when women were enrolled at a large number of all-female medical schools and a few coed medical schools. But as medicine grew more professional, scientific, and prestigious after 1910, the all-women's medical schools were forced to close, and coed medical schools allowed only small numbers of women to

THE CLASS OF 1899, JOHNS HOPKINS SCHOOL OF MEDICINE
BLANCHE NETTLETON EPLER IS SECOND FROM THE END ON THE SECOND ROW (NUMBER 14)
Alan Mason Chesney Medical Archives, Johns Hopkins University

enroll, a policy that lasted until the 1970s.

Increasingly, women physicians like Epler practiced in remote locales such as Hatteras. Outlying communities found recruiting male physicians difficult, and their less rigid, frontier-style society usually left more room for women to emerge as leaders. These communities often showed greater tolerance of nonconformist women in general. Indeed, the Outer Banks had long been renowned for strong women who could handle a fishing boat as well as a frying pan.

As the only physician on Hatteras Island, Epler served both the Coast Guard and the broader community from 1923 to 1925. When Epler arrived aboard the mailboat from Roanoke Island, Mis' Bashi welcomed the doctor into her cottage by Pamlico Sound. They lived together until Epler had her own house built.

From their first meeting, Epler believed that she had found a kindred spirit. She described the seventy-eight-year-old midwife as "comely and agile, her visage one of strength and thought." Sharing cornbread and coconut cake, Mis' Bashi told the lady physician her life story that first night. She was descended from a Devonshire, England, castaway and had gone to school for only five weeks as a girl. Epler noted that Mis' Bashi "had never learned to read, but had been taught to work indoors and out and to spin." She was known, Epler said, as a "couthy woman," an Outer

Banks term for a capable, self-reliant woman.

Mis' Bashi had taken care of others all her life. She had nursed her chronically ill mother for years and raised her younger siblings, her own six children, and her brother's children. "Then for 45 years," Epler wrote, "she ministered to all the sick of the region, a local doctor coming only at rare intervals."

Midwifery was a demanding craft. When a pregnant woman needed her, Mis' Bashi traveled for hours through the hottest summer days and stormiest winter nights. Her sand pony, Napoleon, pulled her in a two-wheeled cart. Mis' Bashi "was smart, exact and knowing," Epler discovered; "she established her own art of medicine and it worked." When Epler asked how she had become such a successful midwife, Mis' Bashi said, "My own mother wit and being mindable to what a good doctor was tellin' me made me fitten to do it."

Mis' Bashi often moved into a mother's home for days or possibly even weeks. Preterm labor or a complicated pregnancy required her to arrive at the bedside early, rather than wait until contractions started, and she probably stayed until the mother was ready to care for the child herself. "Her fee at first was $2.50 for the care of mother and babe," Epler wrote, though "later this became $3 and now $10."

Like nearly all of the historical record, Epler's

National Geographic article is vague about how she and Mis' Bashi actually handled deliveries. We can imagine the pair's skill and ingenuity from other nursing cases that she described in more detail. When a fisherman named Nevada arrived with a stingray tail embedded in his leg, Epler had not yet received her medical instruments from Kalamazoo. She and Mis' Bashi improvised tools out of cut-down lard and coffee cans, then rustled up their own treatment out of turpentine, coal oil, hot water, soap, and Epler's one bottle of Mercurochrome. Stretching the patient across the kitchen table, Epler cut away the stingray's tail, aided, she said, by "Mis' Bashi's 'mother wit' and her nimble, clean hands."

Epler witnessed the last days of traditional childbirth: at home, low-tech, under women's control, tended by a midwife. However, she did not always understand the community's handling of childbirth. When she attended the eighth delivery of a woman named Mrs. Vienner, Epler observed disapprovingly that "a bevy of silent, sitting women, useless and immovable, lined the room and porch." This congregation of women outside Mrs. Vienner's home was an island custom. The father and other men withdrew from the home altogether. The expecting mother's closest female relatives and friends comforted her in the birthing room, while community women waited in silent vigil—sometimes in prayer, some-times just in a quiet gesture of solidarity. I doubt a woman in labor considered them "useless." Mothers themselves, they reminded her that she, too, could make it through the shadow of maternity.

Although Epler failed to understand some of the island's childbearing customs, her medical skills seem to have been appreciated. A few decades earlier, even a Johns Hopkins–educated physician like Epler would have had little to offer Mis' Bashi and Hatteras mothers. But by the 1920s, obstetrical advances—especially the use of anesthesia, new procedures for suturing perineal tears, and an appreciation for aseptic delivery—had made childbirth less perilous and painful. At Hatteras, which had no hospital, Epler and Mis' Bashi delivered babies using elements of both traditional midwifery and modern medicine. But nationwide, midwifery was gradually falling out of favor as childbearing moved into hospitals.

Epler left Hatteras in October 1925 for the Phipps Clinic in Baltimore. She returned to the Outer Banks to practice general medicine in 1929 but found that the "garish lure of 'civilization' had taken its toll." She praised the old islanders like Mis' Bashi for "their willingness to help humanity in every way" but railed against automobiles, the new clubs of wealthy duck hunters, and even the young people's rage for "high heels and rouge, and picture shows."

By 1933, Epler moved away from Mis' Bashi and back to her childhood home in Illinois. For a few brief years, however, the lives of these two women crossed, leaving us an extraordinary portrait of their arduous labors to bring women and children out from the shadow of maternity. United by mutual respect and a commitment to their patients, a modern scientific physician and a traditional healer brought the best of old and new to the Outer Banks.

"A Couthy Woman"

BATHSHEBA FOSTER MAKING LYE AT HATTERAS ISLAND, CIRCA 1925
National Geographic Image Collection

Mis' Bashi stirred about the spacious old brick fireplace, with its crane and firedogs, and brought from the coals an old four-legged skillet in which she had baked a delicious cornbread. Lying on the hearth was a mammoth bushy-tailed, long-haired cat, one of the numerous beautiful descendants of an old island Maltese and a brown, bushy-tailed Norwegian cat that had been the sole survivor of a wreck. Mis' Bashi's fireplace was almost the last of its kind on the island, though there was an older one, with a chimney of hardwood kept washed down with salt to make it noncombustible.

In a worn slab-wood rocker in which my hostess had rocked her six children, I rested after dinner and listened to her tale of a remarkable life history.

What I learned that night and later entitles Mis' Bashi to a place in the annals of medical history. The old nurse belonged to the island's remnant. Her blood, her sterling character, and her beautiful, broad dialect were heritages of the old Devonshire castaway. She was comely and agile, her visage one of strength and thought.

Of only five weeks "schoolin'," she had never learned to read, but had been taught to work indoors and out and to spin. At 16 "out" (old) she married and at 21 "out," in a far Life Service station hamlet, she undertook her first obstetrical case.

"Doctor, I knew nothin' of it; but Mehaley read me a doctor book, and the moon was comin' to full, so the baby would be thrifty. One born in the dark of the moon is not."

On her little plantation, in pine woods by the sound, though widowed later, she cared for a psychiatric mother, raised her own brood and her mother's and her brother's children, cared for cows, pigs, and gardens. Then for 45 years she ministered to all the sick of the region, a local doctor coming only at rare intervals.

Her sand pony Napoleon carried her in a two-wheeled cart through woods and sand and water, in gale or sunshine, to her patients. Often afoot she swung with her Viking stride down beaches or through woods. She was smart, exact, and knowing, though she signed by mark, and she was known as a "couthy" (capable) woman. Her dignity of bearing and courtesy were exquisite. Thus she fell into the role that Nature cast for her.

Months later I realized how her personality, linked with a touch of science, prevented morbid results from household conditions. She established her own art of medicine and it worked. . . .

One midnight I returned from a trip across the sedge to Mis' Landy, whose pain had "swayzed" to the back, the legitimate place to which it might swayze, since by advice of neighbors she refused the operation for gallstones. I had just extinguished my lantern when four men brought in on a sail Mr. Nevada. While fishing on the ocean hours before, the man had been attacked by a sting ray.

More than two inches of stony-spined tail lay imbedded in his leg and three inches protruded.

"Doc," said Mr. Johnnie, "the sting ray is aimin' to kill Nevada, but we traveled him to you. Mr. Daniel died with sting ray and Christopher had to have his leg cut off."

For hours such consolations had been fed to Mr. Nevada.

"Doc, I'm aimin' to die; for, when 30 out, my sins I placed on the Lord for my mansion in the sky."

This piety of the islander, who is an island unto himself, had kept the men from meddling with the wound, but fear and passivity make a poor horse to ride alone. "Mr. Nevada," I said, "courage and spunk and doing exactly as I tell you will save your leg. Now, men, listen: You and I and Mr. Nevada are on this job, and the Lord will work through us."

They listened, astounded.

"Your [sic] not fooling with him will save the leg. It is filled with clean prong and clean sea water. He is not going to lose his leg."

My medical equipment had been so long in sailing somewhere else on the sound that at first I had improvised utensils out of cutdown lard and coffee cans. I made my own sterile dressings and found that hot water and soap, turpentine and coal oil, and my one bottle of Dr. Hugh Young's then recent mercurochrome served me well.

We placed Mr. Nevada on Mis' Bashi's kitchen table. Mis' Bashi's "mother wit" and her nimble, clean hands aided as the villainous prong was cut away, and the red medicine filled the wound. The color won over the men to me, for to them medical science meant nothing compared to the drug stuff of general store.

"Madam," said Mr. Nevada, "I'm some proud to know you, and you needn't want to go without a home. Cynthy's house, which you aim to buy, I'll see you get."

With the customary adieu, "Come go home with me," they left.

That sting-ray wound was to me a blessing in disguise; for I had spent futile hours trying to buy a cottage. It was the quaint custom of islanders not to sell land from their large family tracts, or rent or sell houses! Neither lumber and tools nor carpenter could be obtained to build me a home, and Cynthy's cottage, which "rested on blocks because of toids," was alluring.

From Blanch Nettleton Epler,
"A Bit of Elizabethan England in America,"
National Geographic (1933)

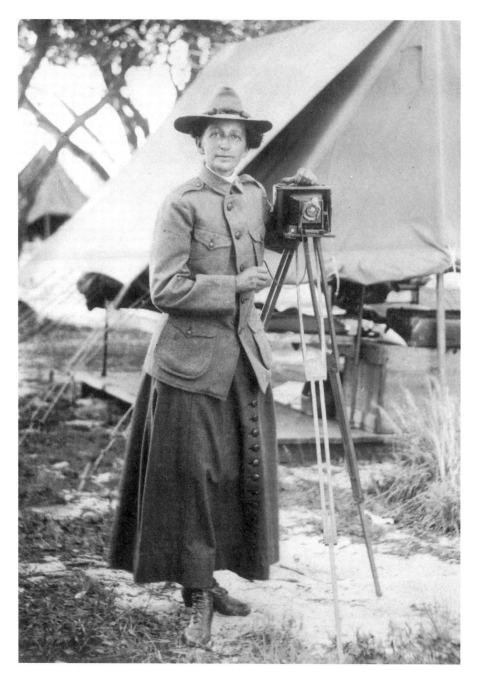

BAYARD WOOTTEN AT WORK
North Carolina Collection, University of North Carolina Library at Chapel Hill

LIGHT AND AIR

B ayard Wootten has long been one of my favorite photographers. Born in New Bern in 1875, she ran portrait studios in New Bern and Chapel Hill for nearly half a century. She was both a talented studio photographer and a gifted pictorialist with an artist's eye. She went anywhere, anytime, to get a good photograph. Camera in hand, she stayed for days in an Appalachian logging camp, flew in a Wright brothers' airplane, prowled the Croatan swamps.

A splendid book, *Light and Air: The Photography of Bayard Wootten*, introduces Wootten's life and work to this generation. Written by Jerry Cotten, the photographic archivist at the North Carolina Collection at the University of North Carolina at Chapel Hill, the book has much to say about tidewater life early in the twentieth century.

Light and Air focuses on Wootten's photographs of the Great Depression. They stand in sharp contrast to the better-known pictures made by the photographers of the Farm Security Administration (FSA), a New Deal agency charged with documenting rural hardship. Full of pathos and hopelessness, the FSA photographs are the most enduring images of America in the 1930s. *Let Us Now Praise Famous Men*, by James Agee and Walker Evans, contains probably the best-known photographs of that ilk: stark images of hollow-eyed Alabama tenant farmers living dreary, poverty-stricken lives.

FSA photographers such as Walker Evans and Dorothea Lange had the most profound influence on American documentary photography in the twentieth century. But while their photographs inspired pity, they rarely meant much to Southerners. That was not because people in the South failed to recognize the FSA's harsh images of the Great Depression. Rare was the rural Southern family that did not know poverty and privation in those years. Rather, few Southerners, black or white, recognized the one-dimensional view of their lives and the bleakness of the human spirit portrayed in the FSA photographs.

Wootten saw a different South. Her photographs do not ignore the hardships of the Great Depression. She does not conceal ragged clothes,

dilapidated homes, and the gauntness of so many of the people whom she photographed. But my favorites among Wootten's photographs go far beyond social criticism; they depict a hard-pressed people mustering the grace and strength to survive the Great Depression.

Look, for instance, at the 1937 photograph of the girl taking a break from picking strawberries. She was one of many seasonal workers who migrated every spring to Chadbourn, in Columbus County, to labor in the fields. Though no longer the world's largest strawberry market, as it

HARVESTING TULIPS AT PINETOWN (BEAUFORT COUNTY), 1930S
North Carolina Collection, University of North Carolina Library at Chapel Hill

STRAWBERRY PICKER, CHADBOURN (COLUMBUS COUNTY), 1930S
North Carolina Collection, University of North Carolina Library at Chapel Hill

had been from 1895 to 1905, Chadbourn still attracted pickers from all over southeastern North Carolina.

To say that this photograph ignores the girl's plight because she looks so content—as many defenders of the FSA school of documentary photography might—misses Wootten's point entirely. In fact, you cannot miss the signs of the girl's hard life: her frayed dress full of holes, the missing buttons, the ragged shawl, her work-worn hands. Wootten's home-state audience was all too familiar with that sort of soul-wrenching poverty,

and it would also have known that, being in Chadbourn, the girl was from a family in far direr straits than most. But what stands out in Wootten's photograph is, of course, the girl's glowing spirit rising above all that misfortune.

Look, too, at the photograph of Ben Owen turning a pot in Jugtown, in Moore County, in the 1930s. For ages, craftsmen had been making pottery out of the central Piedmont's crude red clay. They lived in a hard, unforgiving region of the state for farming, where the clay soil was more curse than boon. But potters like Owen took what

FISHERMAN MENDING NETS
North Carolina Collection, University of North Carolina Library at Chapel Hill

A HISTORIAN'S COAST

BEN OWEN, JUGTOWN, 1930s
North Carolina Collection, University of North Carolina Library at Chapel Hill

little the land gave them—the clay—and created breathtakingly beautiful shapes and glazes. Wootten's genius was to catch Owen at just that moment when the plain and glorious seemed like one and the same thing.

Finally, look closely at the young black laborer standing in a tobacco field. You know that he has worked in brutally hot, humid weather since sunrise. His fingers ache from cropping tobacco. The leaf nicotine stings his skin. His feet hurt. Notice, though, how he holds himself and wears his tattered trousers; he is the picture of verve and

TOBACCO HARVESTER
North Carolina Collection, University of North Carolina Library at Chapel Hill

APPALACHIAN FIDDLER, 1930s
North Carolina Collection, University of North Carolina Library at Chapel Hill

vim and insouciant joy. Wootten has captured a strength of spirit that cannot be confined to that tobacco field. Hard times will not hold that young fellow down.

That is what Wootten was ultimately saying: people could rise above the Great Depression and even above what one of my favorite novelists, Robertson Davies, once called that "underlying, deep grief of things." They could do it right here, in this place, out of their own hearts, with their own two hands. The FSA photographers never saw it, never believed people had it in them. They saw merely the hard red clay of Depression-era lives. Wootten saw how North Carolina's people turned that clay into the human equivalent of Jugtown pottery—that is, into lives of quiet grace and, sometimes, iridescent beauty.

HORSE TRADERS
North Carolina Collection, University of North Carolina Library at Chapel Hill

BEHIND THE VEIL

T he stories told by our elders bring the past to life in ways that history books rarely can. This may be truest of the African American past in coastal towns like New Bern, where few written records or historical sites shed light on a black population that was for many years the local majority. Through the memories of African American elders, we can revisit the influenza epidemic of 1919, the maraudings of the Ku Klux Klan, and the birth of the civil-rights movement. Vacant tenant houses and abandoned tobacco farms come back to life, and the displaced victims of the great fire of 1922 are finally heard. When a ninety-six-year-old New Bern man tells stories about his slave parents, even the era of human bondage can seem like yesterday.

These stories are brought to light in "Behind the Veil: Documenting African American Life in the Jim Crow South," an exciting and revealing oral-history project undertaken by Duke University's Center for Documentary Studies. In 1992, graduate students from Duke, the University of North Carolina at Chapel Hill, North Carolina Central University, and other Southern universities began interviewing an astonishing twelve hundred African Americans from Virginia to Mississippi. Among them were more than seventy elderly men and women who grew up along the North Carolina coast.

Recently, I had the opportunity to review the "Behind the Veil" interviews for New Bern and Craven County. Much of the collection still has to be cataloged, indexed, and transcribed. But I introduced the project's directors—professors, Raymond Gavins, William Chafe, and Robert Korstad—to many of the interviewees in Craven County, and they showed their gratitude by opening the collection for my historical research.

The interviews focus on the period of Southern history called the Jim Crow era. Named for an antebellum minstrel act that amounted to a racist parody of African Americans, Jim Crow was the system of American apartheid that prevailed from the 1890s until the civil-rights movement of the 1960s.

The forced separation of black and white people was the cornerstone of Jim Crow. "I went to a black church, I had black friends, I lived in a black neighborhood," Ronald White of New Bern told a Duke interviewer. "The only time I had contact with white people was when I went downtown with my father." New Bern's schools, hospitals, graveyards, theaters, restaurants, trolleys, and buses—even its water fountains and swimming beaches—were segregated by race.

"You were not even allowed in a restroom in the bus station," recalled Dorcas E. Carter, a retired teacher born in New Bern in 1913. "That got to be devastating."

A black man who defied Jim Crow risked his livelihood and put his life in jeopardy. If he insisted on sitting near the front of a bus or tried to order a drink at a soda fountain, he was bound at least for the "Black Maria," the police paddy wagon. He might lose his job, have his credit revoked, or face a visit from the Ku Klux Klan.

But the "Behind the Veil" interviews reveal that Jim Crow demanded more than racial segregation. It also demanded an outward show of total deference. The Ku Klux Klan—"the businessmen from downtown," a New Bern woman's father explained to her—terrorized blacks for the simplest things, like coming to the front door of a white family's house instead of the back or not yielding to a white person on a sidewalk.

A black man could not even look a white man in the eye. "They would put a black man in jail for direct eyeballing," remembered the Reverend William Hickman, who was born and raised at Hickman Hill, a small community off Highway 70 between New Bern and Havelock.

African Americans also faced risks if they showed their intelligence in ways that upstaged whites. Several interviewees remembered a black physician who was driven from New Bern after he healed a white patient. Black doctors usually were not allowed to examine whites, but this man's wife insisted that the black physician, a recent graduate of a prestigious medical school, see her husband after the town's white doctors could not

Dorcas E. Carter, retired school teacher and survivor of the great fire of 1922, at her home in New Bern

Photograph by Scott Taylor

heal him. The black physician's medical skill meant his exile.

Many interviewees described farm life under Jim Crow. Sharecropping, the lot of most black farmers, often seemed like slavery. Bessie Spicer, an eighty-year-old New Bern resident, recalled how her family sharecropped at Wyse Fork near Kinston. After her stepfather died, she ran the farm with her mother and sisters. No matter how many "sunups to sundowns" they sweated in the fields, they always owed "the man" at year's end.

Debt peonage was a way of life. "What the boss man said, went," Spicer stated matter-of-factly. Her family had to buy groceries at a commissary owned by the landlord, who insisted that children work in the fields as a requirement for living in his tenant houses. Spicer's schooling stopped at the fourth grade. And when her family settled its accounts with the landlord after the tobacco harvest, Jim Crow decreed that they dare not question his accounting.

Poverty was a fact of life. To go to church, Spicer recalled, family members borrowed clothes "from the boss lady." They had to return those clothes before dinner.

These oral histories portray much more than Jim Crow's hardships and perils. They also describe quiet struggles for dignity and equality, stories of perseverance and faith and triumph. Most of the elderly black men and women interviewed by the students remembered tight-knit families, caring neighborhoods, and strong churches that helped them survive. "We had a lot of love," explained Clarita Wordlaw, later a leader of the civil-rights movement in New Bern. Many also recalled with great pride the local African American schools, especially the West Street School in New Bern.

Several things surprised me in the "Behind the Veil" interviews. One was how often rural black and white people defied Jim Crow by having friendships that crossed racial lines. Janie Williams, a seventy-six-year-old woman who grew up in Pitt County, was typical. During her early married life on a Clayroot tenant farm, she and a white tenant woman alternated fixing supper for their two families. They shared a dinner table, traded farm work, and cared for each other's children. "It was like a big family, everybody working and living together," she recalled. Not even Jim Crow could build a wall high enough to keep people apart all the time.

I was also surprised at how many of the black families in New Bern had roots on the Outer Banks. Dorcas E. Carter, for instance, described in loving detail her grandmother, a fisher-woman who had grown up on Portsmouth Island. By the late 1800s, her grandmother had moved to New Bern and brought her skiff and fishing nets with her. "She would go up the river every day," Carter remembered. "She would take my brothers, and they would come back with crabs and fish."

No event is more prominent in the "Behind the Veil" interviews than the great fire of 1922. Before December 1, 1922, New Bern was home to one of the most prosperous black middle-class communities in the American South. The neighborhood of skilled black artisans and professional people was centered on George Street near St. Peter's African Methodist Episcopal Zion Church, the mother church of the AME Zion denomination in the South. Interviewees recalled the community's many black-owned businesses, its paved streets and gaslights, the beauty of old St. Peter's, and the trolley that could be ridden downtown for only five cents.

Carter remembered it well. "To me," she told a Duke student, "I felt as though we were almost like the historic section of New Bern. The houses were very historic and the people dressed so modest, so cultured. You could see the men escorting

ST. PETER'S AFRICAN METHODIST EPISCOPAL ZION CHURCH, NEW BERN, AFTER THE GREAT FIRE OF 1922
New Bern Fireman's Museum Collection, New Bern-Craven County Public Library

PANORAMA OF THE RED CROSS TENT CITY FOR VICTIMS OF THE NEW BERN FIRE OF 1922
Steve Jones Collection, New Bern-Craven County Public Library

CHARRED RUINS OF HOMES IN NEW BERN AFTER THE GREAT FIRE OF 1922
New Bern Fireman's Museum Collection, New Bern-Craven County Public Library

the ladies by the arm, all dressed with their walking canes and their derbies. It glowed. . . . People would come out looking graceful and dignified. Then the big fire came and destroyed this."

The great fire of 1922 incinerated the entire community and left more than three thousand black citizens homeless. For reasons that remain unclear, New Bern's town leaders condemned the burned-over streets and took the land despite black protests. A cemetery, ballparks, and a police station displaced the black community. Impoverished, many of the former residents moved to New York City or to makeshift camps on the edge of New Bern. "I always wondered why we could never go back," Carter said. "This was a turning point in my life."

The "Behind the Veil" collection holds hundreds of no less important stories, but I would like to conclude with a much smaller, more personal incident. It has to do with the sort of history that is engraved in hearts, not history books. It is a Civil War tale told by Annie Gavins, a New Bern resident born in 1913. Gavins grew up with her great-grandmother Hannah, who had been born a slave in Swansboro, a fishing village thirty miles south of New Bern.

"My great-grandmother told the experience of having seen Abraham Lincoln in Swansboro," Gavins said. "He came to their plantation. He was asking the stable boy questions [about] how he was faring. He was by himself. He was well dressed and had nice horses. He was tall. All of this I remember. After he went back to Washington, that's when they started laying the plans to free the slaves. You see, he came to see how things were before he signed the [Emancipation] Proclamation."

The history books say that President Lincoln

never visited North Carolina during the Civil War, but I do not think any historian could shake Gavins's faith in her great-grandmother's story. I could not help but be impressed by her careful attention to detail, and I heard the conviction in her voice. I am also aware that hundreds of former slaves across the South told similarly unexplainable stories about meeting the Great Emancipator.

Personally, I would never try to convince Annie Gavins that her great-grandmother did not meet Lincoln. Who am I to tell a woman of eighty years what is possible and what is not? I know all too well that there is more than one sort of his-tory. There is history that can be chronicled in books, celebrated in parades, preserved in muse-ums. And then there is another history, one with which we are all acquainted; it is more private, less noisy, and far less craving of public recogni-tion. I like to think of it as a history of the heart: of hopes and prayers, of hurts and disappoint-ments, of loves and tendernesses that are never forgotten. We all know that this sort of history is as real as anything in books and museums, and I have found few better places to look for it than the "Behind the Veil" interviews.

RACHEL CARSON AT BIRD SHOAL

I enjoy chaperoning school trips to Bird Shoal, a marshy island just across Taylor Creek from Beaufort. The children are excited to learn outdoors. They scurry among the tidal pools, pelting their teachers with dozens of questions about seashore life. Amid the clamor, I am always reminded of a quiet, solitary young woman who waded in those tidal pools half a century before us.

Long before she was famous, Rachel Carson visited Bird Shoal. Her best-selling books about the sea lay years ahead of her. She had not yet dreamed of changing history with *Silent Spring*, her trailblazing exposé on the dangers of DDT (dichloro-diphenyl-trichloroethane) and other pesticides. At Bird Shoal, she was an obscure young biologist discovering the mysteries of the sea. She wandered the island in peace, ankle deep in marsh mud and entranced by the beauty of whelks and sea anemones.

I find it fitting that Rachel Carson National Estuarine Research Reserve, which includes Bird Shoal, bears this shy, soft-spoken biologist's name—and not only because she wrote such wonderful books about the sea's ecology. Carson had a special fondness for the North Carolina coast. She visited Bird Shoal frequently when she was a young woman, and she also kept a special place in her heart for Lake Mattamuskeet, in Hyde County, only a few miles from Pamlico Sound. Though she made only one visit to Lake Mattamuskeet, she continued to tell her friends about the experience for more than a decade.

Imagining Carson at Bird Shoal, I have often wondered how a woman so private and so absorbed in scientific study came to write one of the boldest indictments of humanity's mistreatment of the earth. But looking more closely at her coastal sojourns here in North Carolina, I think that we can glimpse the inspiration for *Silent Spring*

Carson was born in 1907 in the Allegheny Valley of Pennsylvania. Encouraged in her love of the outdoors by her mother, she studied marine biology at Johns Hopkins University and the Woods Hole Marine Laboratory. Until she was able to make a living as a writer in 1952, she worked as an aquatic biologist and editor for the United States Fish and Wildlife Service.

I do not know exactly when Carson first visited the North Carolina coast, but she had certainly explored the Beaufort vicinity by 1940. Her first book, *Under the Sea Wind*, was published in the fall of 1941 and opened with a long evocation of a May evening at Beaufort's Town Marsh and Bird Shoal.

Carson's prose brings that spring night to life. Shad burst through Beaufort Inlet. A black skimmer rests after a long flight from the Yucatan. Newborn diamondback terrapins slip into the dark waters of Back Sound. And—in a passage I have remembered since I first read it as a teenager—a marsh rat catches "the scent of terrapin and terrapin eggs, . . . heavy in the air." The rat devours one of the eggs, then, blinded by gluttony, is speared by a blue heron.

In *Under the Sea Wind*, Carson first displayed the rare combination of literary grace and scientific accuracy that would mark all her writing. Overlooked in the upheaval of World War II, however, the book received little attention and sold poorly. Not until ten years later, after *The Sea Around Us* was published to great acclaim, did Carson's first book also become a national bestseller.

Soon after World War II, Carson toured Lake Mattamuskeet to prepare a booklet called *Mattamuskeet: A National Wildlife Refuge* for the United States Fish and Wildlife Service. Purchased by the federal government in 1934 for a waterfowl sanctuary, Lake Mattamuskeet attracted one of the largest assemblies of Canada geese and whistling swans on the Atlantic seaboard. Between forty thousand and sixty thousand Canadas and between five thousand and ten thousand swans wintered on the lake, as did great flocks of pintails, widgeons, black ducks, mallards, and green- and blue-winged teals.

When visiting Lake Mattamuskeet, Carson stayed at the old pumping station at New Holland, a little village on the lake's southern shore.

RACHEL CARSON WADING ASHORE AT CHINCOTEAGUE NATIONAL WILDLIFE REFUGE, VIRGINIA, 1946

Photograph by Shirley Briggs, Courtesy of Rachel Carson History Project

The pumps had been used in a failed plan to drain and farm the lake in the 1920s. The Civilian Conservation Corps, a New Deal agency, converted the station into a hunting lodge with a circular staircase that ascended an old smokestack 120 feet to a wildlife observation post.

Her visit to Hyde County made a deep impression on Carson. Her letters to her closest friend, Dorothy Freeman, have recently been published in *Always, Rachel*, which was edited by Freeman's granddaughter, Martha Freeman. Carson first wrote to Freeman about Lake Mattamuskeet on October 17, 1959. "I hope I can take you to Lake Mattamuskeet in North Carolina. . . . I'll

---

"The Constant, Haunting Music of the Geese"

Rachel Carson to Dorothy Freeman, October 17, 1959

Somewhere in my own little notebooks there is a record of those morning waterfowl flights as I observed them several years ago—Fall of '56, it must have been. . . . What impressed me so was the reverse pattern of flights in gulls and waterfowl. The gulls toward the open sea at sunset, but upstream in the morning—the ducks and geese just the reverse. Of course I imagine that the evening flights of waterfowl are always new migrants from the north, and that those seen heading down the bay in the morning are resuming the southward journey.

Sometime, somehow, I hope I can take you to Lake Mattamuskeet in North Carolina. That experience was something I'll never forget—the countless thousands of Canada geese wintering there. During the evening and—I seem to remember—even far into the night, the throbbing chorus of their voices rose from the lake where they were resting. But the greatest thrill came when we went out just before sunrise to watch the flocks rising up and heading out into the neighboring fields where they forage by day. They would pass literally just over our heads—so low the sunshine made their dark heads and necks look

like brown velvet. And all the while the air filled with their music.

Now I'd give a lot just to have one small **V** of them pass over here!

Rachel Carson to Dorothy Freeman, November 1963

You ask where Mattamuskeet is. In North Carolina, inland a bit from Pamlico Sound—a large, shallow, fresh water lake. Somewhere I ought to have some copies of the gov't bulletin I wrote about it. If I can find any I'll send you one. The thing I always remember about it is the constant, haunting music of the geese—thousands and thousands of them. I think M. [Mattamuskeet] is the largest wintering ground for the Canadas. Snow geese go to Pea Island, above Hatteras. Also at M., I remember the huge flocks of myrtle warblers, most appropriate in the numerous myrtle bushes, along with many other small birds. When . . . I went (probably late 40's) it was a good day's drive from here. Now with many new highways, and bypasses around Richmond, etc., it would be much less. Want to go?

From Martha Freeman, editor, *Always, Rachel: The Letters of Rachel Carson and Dorothy Freeman, 1952–1964: The Story of a Remarkable Friendship* (Boston: Beacon Press, 1996)

THE OLD PUMPING STATION AT LAKE MATTAMUSKEET, CIRCA 1930.
North Carolina Collection, University of North Carolina Library at Chapel Hill

never forget . . . the countless thousands of Canada geese wintering there," she said. "During the evening and—I seem to remember—even far into the night, the throbbing chorus of their voices rose from the lake where they were resting. But the greatest thrill came when we went out just before sunrise to watch the flocks rising up and heading out into the neighboring fields where they forage by day. They would pass literally just over our heads—so low the sunshine made their dark heads and necks look like brown velvet. And all the while the air filled with their music."

Six months before her death, in a November 1963 letter, Carson wrote Freeman again about Lake Mattamuskeet, recalling "the constant, haunting music of the geese."

Carson returned to Bird Shoal in June 1951. She had just written *The Sea Around Us*, which made her an international celebrity. That stunning portrait of the world's oceans was translated into thirty-two languages and remained on the bestseller list for eighty-six weeks, a record at the time. In Beaufort, Carson sought solitude at what she called her "favorite beach." She spent her days "getting acquainted with a whole village of sea anemones . . . [and] wading around in water up to my knees, not a human soul in sight."

It was in her next book, *The Edge of the Sea*, that Carson introduced by name the site of her se-

cluded excursions in North Carolina. "To visit Bird Shoal," she wrote, "one goes out by boat through channels winding through the Town Marsh of Beaufort." Thousands of fiddler crabs greeted the visitor, Carson observed, and she likened the "sound of so many small chitinous feet" to "the crackling of paper."

Carson saw beauty in the least of Bird Shoal's creatures. She marveled at the "mysterious forces of creation" at work in the long, twisted strand of a whelk's egg sac. She tracked a horseshoe crab across a mud flat and exposed a toadfish concealed in eelgrass. She divulged the telltale tentacles of a sand anemone searching the waves for detritus and the "protruding chimneys" of the plumed worm Diopatra.

Carson had become one of the most popular writers in America. Her articles about sea life appeared regularly in magazines as diverse as *Life*, *Audubon*, and *Woman's Home Companion*. She had received the highest honors awarded to writers and scientists. Many people would have rested on their laurels. Carson could surely have spent more days by her beloved seashore.

But *The Edge of the Sea* was Carson's last book about the ocean. By the late 1950s, a large body of scientific evidence had accumulated about the dangerous effects on living organisms of DDT and other organic pesticides made of chlorinated

RACHEL CARSON IN LABORATORY, WOODS HOLE OCEANOGRAPHIC INSTITUTE, 1953
FROM AN ARTICLE IN THE NEW BEDFORD, MA *STANDARD TIMES*
Courtesy of Rachel Carson History Project

hydrocarbons. This information remained widely scattered, had not yet reached the general public, and was not taken seriously by government and industry. The pesticides were still used with little restraint or public oversight.

As one of the few popular writers with the expertise to sift through complex scientific data, Carson believed it was her duty to expose the dangers of the chemical agents that, developed mainly for use during World War II, had become part of daily life.

Carson had been troubled by atomic bomb testing in the Pacific Ocean, but she was not a protester. Privately, though, she had grave reservations about science's new threats to the earth. "It was comforting to suppose," she wrote Freeman in February 1958, "that the stream of life would flow on through time in whatever course that God had appointed it—without interference by one of the drops of the stream—man."

Until *Silent Spring*, Carson used her fame mainly to encourage parents to nurture in children a sense of wonder at the natural world. She still felt more at home at Bird Shoal than in a bully pulpit. She did not relish controversy, and she was not at heart a political person.

Yet Carson never hesitated when it came to *Silent Spring*, not even when she was diagnosed with cancer in 1960. She studied more than a thousand scientific papers. She consulted with the world's leading entomologists, chemists, and ecologists. When she put pen to paper, Carson brandished her facts—to borrow the words of the old hymn—like a terrible swift sword.

Published in 1962, *Silent Spring* revealed how pesticides accumulated in the food chain, damaging birds, fish, and even humans. It was a stunning achievement and an overnight sensation. Not in ages had a scientific work sparked such widespread public debate—or such bitter repudiations.

"The 'control of nature,'" Carson wrote, "is a phrase conceived in arrogance, born of the Neanderthal age of biology and philosophy. . . . It is our alarming misfortune that so primitive a science has armed itself with the most modern and terrible weapons, and that in turning them against insects it has also turned them against the Earth."

Not surprisingly, the chemical industry was the harshest critic of *Silent Spring*. A Chicago chemical company sought to have the book suppressed by the courts. The industry devoted a fortune to its attempt to discredit Carson and make her appear a "hysterical woman." Daunted by the controversy, several magazines, including *Reader's Digest*, backed out of their agreements to publish excerpts of *Silent Spring*. One sympathetic critic called it the most vilified book since Charles Darwin's *On the Origin of Species*.

Despite the chemical industry's attacks, *Silent Spring* met enthusiastic praise from most scientists and became a worldwide bestseller. A year later, President Kennedy's Science Advisory Committee issued a detailed report substantiating Carson's claims. Confronted by public outrage, the United States and other world governments enacted important reforms governing the use of pesticides. *Silent Spring* inspired a sweeping ecological consciousness and became one of the most influential books of the twentieth century.

Where did Carson find the moral courage to write *Silent Spring*? The sources of such courage are by their nature mysterious, deep, perhaps unknowable. Yet I suspect that the origin of *Silent Spring* lay, ultimately, in her quiet hours of getting to know Bird Shoal, Lake Mattamuskeet, and places like them. By those quiet shores, Carson gained a knowledge of the sea's life that led to an empathy and a sense of interconnectedness with the natural world. I do not believe she could stand idly by when something she knew so intimately and cared for so deeply was threatened.

That is why I believe in exposing children to our coast, and why I give my highest praise to our dedicated science teachers and marine educators. When they introduce children to the seashore, they offer them a chance to discover more than arcane facts of marine biology. They teach them about the glories of all life and give them the opportunity to explore their own humanity and its place among the creatures of the world. I do not see anything that could be more important. And who knows which child on a school trip to Bird Shoal—or Masonboro Island or Merchants Millpond—is the next Rachel Carson?

GOSHEN'S LAND

*You shall live in the region of Goshen
and be near me—you, your children and
grandchildren, your flocks and herds, and all
you have.*

Genesis 45:10

As I drive east on Highway 58, the last landmark before the community of Goshen is the E. E. Bell farm. A long avenue of oaks and cedars veils an antebellum manor house with Classical Revival columns. Now on the National Register of Historic Places, the two-thousand-acre cotton plantation once belonged to James C. Bryan, Jones County's largest planter. The main house is best known for having a crystal chandelier that once hung in the Confederate White House in Richmond, Virginia. The farm's cotton fields crowd Goshen against the Trent River and a little stream called Goshen Branch.

People in Goshen invited me there as a histo-

rian because the town of Pollocksville, a mile east, intended to build its sewage-treatment plant in this African American farming community. The sewage plant would spray its sludge only a few feet away from the Goshen cemetery and would take some of the last black-owned farmland in Jones County. Goshen was also one of the black communities settled immediately after the Civil War. The more famous town of Princeville, seventy miles north of Goshen, was the first incorporated African American town in the United States, but Goshen and a number of other, mostly disappearing rural black communities, were founded in the same time period. Goshen's residents believed their community deserved historic recognition and saw the building of the sewage plant as "an act of desecration," as one lady there told me. They also feared that the waste odors and runoff would pollute their forests and streams.

When I travel through the small towns and remote byways of tidewater North Carolina, I see a growing number of communities like Goshen that seem to be in the way of "progress." As more and more people move to the Carolina coast, and as growing numbers of tourists visit our beaches, many older, usually poor communities are threatened by the construction of sewage plants, highways, bridges, and waste-disposal sites. No place seems sacred. And to me, as a historian, many of these developments seem bent on erasing the past.

The citizens of Goshen hoped that if I could help them document the historical significance of their community, they might be able to pressure Pollocksville's leaders into not building the sewage plant there. I knew this would not be easy. When I drove the dirt road to pick up Hattie Brown at her farmhouse, I already knew that finding historical documents on the African American past was exceedingly difficult.

On my way to Goshen, I had stopped at the North Carolina State Archives in Raleigh to search for written records on the community's past. I had also paused to ransack the Jones County Courthouse in Trenton. I had found a few relevant deeds, an old list of local slaves, and a few other documents, but not much. I had no idea how much I would learn in Goshen—not just about coastal history, but about the meaning of history and what is worth preserving.

In a pine grove by the branch, Hattie Brown and I walked among Goshen's dead. A soft-spoken sixty-seven-year-old, Mrs. Brown recalled all the departed, whether buried in unmarked graves or under marble headstones. She had at least a few words for every soul. I listened while she wove together the threads of Goshen's past for me.

Hattie Brown learned Goshen's history from her grandmother Luvenia Smith Loftin. A midwife and lay doctor, Luvenia forbade her descendants to forget Goshen's past. What Mrs. Brown told me, Luvenia had taught her.

Born a slave in 1848, Luvenia grew up on Richard Oldfield's plantation on the White Oak River, about ten miles south of Goshen. Her father, Luke Smith, rebelled against the wealthy cotton planter. He secretly gardened in the nearby woods. He taught Luvenia to read by slipping books from Oldfield's library. He led clandestine prayer meetings. He also ran away many times. Luvenia saw him maimed with a bullwhip yet still disappear back into the woods.

In 1863, after Union troops drove Confederate forces out of most coastal towns, Luke Smith and his wife, Melissa, led their children to freedom. To reach Union-occupied New Bern, they crossed two rivers and the Lakes Pocosin—now a part of Croatan National Forest. It was a wilderness crawling with cottonmouths and alligators. Fourteen-year-old Luvenia barely kept up and nearly drowned fording the Trent River.

Luvenia later married William Loftin, a former slave from Lenoir County. They sharecropped at first. But in the 1870s, they joined the Jordans, the Bests, and other Loftins in purchasing a remote, swampy woodland called "the Goshen tract." Wild plums, not pines, shaded the graveyard in those days.

Together, the families cleared the land by hand, grubbing enough earth for cotton, corn, and sweet potato fields. They raised hogs. They mortgaged everything to buy seed and a mule. A single crop failure could have left them homeless.

Few locales posed more dangers to black landowners than Jones County. During Reconstruction, the Ku Klux Klan terrorized the county's black majority. Years later, the county's most famous son, future United States senator Furnifold Simmons, led the state's white-supremacy movement, which took the right to vote away from black citizens across North Carolina. I had no-

ticed that a portrait of Senator Simmons still graced the main entrance to the Jones County Courthouse.

Amid that racial strife, Goshen was a rare sanctuary. Reached only by an old Indian trail, the community was very secluded. Luvenia freely roamed the forest for her herbal cures. The children played without inhibition. And at Christmas, the people wandered by every home to share good food and glad tidings. Everybody knew everybody, and the community looked out for its own. Only when walking past Pollocksville to the Garnett Heights school did Goshen's children suffer racial taunts.

After Luvenia Loftin's death in 1941, her descendants struggled to hold on to Goshen. Like all small farmers, they suffered from bad weather, feeble mules, and low prices. But Jim Crow also prohibited them from challenging corrupt merchants and produce buyers. And the county sheriff showed little mercy to black farmers delinquent in their tax payments. Hattie Brown remembered all too well when her cousin Laura's family was dispossessed; the family stayed for years in a drafty tobacco barn, and Laura soon died of pneumonia.

We walked past small plastic signs marking the evicted family's graves. "They lived with so many heartaches," Mrs. Brown sighed.

To hold on to the land, Goshen's citizens worked off as well as on the farm. The men traveled to distant sawmills and logging jobs. The women and children picked tobacco on farms owned by white families. In spring, they harvested strawberries a hundred miles away and rushed home on weekends to tend their own farms.

Holding a family together was a feat. For years after their father died, Hattie Brown and her sister Minzelle Dillahunt ran the Loftin farm by themselves. They plowed fields and fought off merchants who tried to take advantage of two women doing "men's work." Their brothers Lucius Jr. and William staved off foreclosure by sending military paychecks home. Sister Leora Murray, a Philadelphia nurse, helped out when she could.

Black-owned farmland dwindled away elsewhere in Jones County, and indeed throughout the coastal plain. When a blacktop replaced the Indian trail in 1952, Goshen's citizens began to commute to domestic and factory jobs in other counties; Jones County itself never offered more than farm work, except for little cut-and-sew factories that went in and out of business every few years. Mrs. Brown's cousin Julia was like many. For decades, she cooked for a white family in Kinston, twenty miles away. She came home only on weekends, but she kept her land in Goshen nonetheless.

Then the drowning of Minzelle's young son in 1956, followed by a great flood in 1957, nearly shattered the community.

Yet Goshen has somehow survived. Today, African Americans comprise 43 percent of Jones County's population, yet they own less than 3 percent of the land. More than half the county's farmers—landowners, tenants, and sharecroppers—were African Americans two generations ago. Now, only a handful of black farmers till the land, and most only raise a few hogs or tend a few acres.

In Jones County, as in many parts of eastern North Carolina, landlessness has led to widespread poverty and hopelessness. Hordes of other black farm people have moved to cities. In the old days, they moved to Brooklyn and New Jersey and Baltimore. Nowadays, they usually do not have to go as far to find opportunity, but the result is the same back home: rural churches with dwindling congregations, elderly people living alone, high rates of alcohol and drug abuse.

But in Goshen, land ownership has meant independence, strong roots, and an enduring closeness to the soil. Hattie Brown can look out her home's windows across cornfields and collard patches that have been in her family for generations. She can see the homes of nieces and nephews, brothers and cousins on the far side of those fields. And thanks to Goshen's deep roots, the children who leave home often do well. Goshen boasts teachers, lawyers, engineers, and scientists among its children. One of Mrs. Brown's nieces I later met is Professor Elvira Williams, who teaches at North Carolina Agricultural and Technical State University in Greensboro. Professor Williams was one of the first African American physicists in the country.

All of this made me ponder the meaning of history and what merits historic recognition. As I got to know Goshen the day when Hattie Brown and I strolled through the cemetery and during later visits, I noticed that young Goshenites have been coming home more often recently. They have returned to join the struggle to save the community and preserve its cemetery and farmland. None of the old homes and local landmarks in Goshen are the sort that will be given protected status by the National Register for Historic Places, like the E. E. Bell farm up the road and the old Foscue Plantation house across the Trent River.

These young people in Goshen seem to know—or at least to intuit, as I did that autumn afternoon in Goshen's cemetery—that the real meaning of history has little to do with antique chandeliers and Doric columns. Mrs. Brown and her neighbors taught me that other things are far more important: the collective experiences of a community and the stories passed from generation to generation by women like Luvenia Loftin and Hattie Brown.

"She Meant Us Never to Forget"

I was told by my grandmother, Luvenia, that she was freed when she was 14 years old. She was born in 1848, at Richard Oldfield's plantation in White Oak, a little settlement out of Maysville. I knew her for a long time. Granddaddy died in 1927, and Luvenia came to live with us here in Goshen. That's when she told us most of the stories about slavery. My father would be working off somewhere, mostly logging, and my mother would be in the fields with the larger children. My little brother and I would be with my grandmother.

My grandmother mentioned many, many things about growing up under slavery. At the Oldfields', they were cleaning up new places to farm. They would dig up trees, getting more and more land ready to be cleared. That was extremely hard work, I know it was. The women would plow and keep the children, see that everything was right around the house. Luvenia did a lot of baby-sitting. They also grew cotton. They had to be out early, stay out late, and they had to keep moving steady.

My grandmother's daddy was named Luke Smith. They called him Pardee. He would run away a whole lot of the time, she said. Luke would get upset and go away. Then

HATTIE BROWN IN THE GOSHEN CEMETERY

Photograph by Chris Seward, courtesy of the Raleigh News and Observer

they would put out a search party till they found him, bring him back and whip him. This happened many, many times, but he would always do it again.

The last time, he got a real bad whipping, but he ran away again and he stayed longer this time. He didn't come back to the plantation.

They got upset because Luke was one of the best working slaves. Finally, his master promised Luvenia's mother, Melissa, that he wouldn't whip Luke anymore if she would go get him back. I don't know how Melissa arranged it, but she contacted him, and they didn't whip him anymore.

That was just before they got free. That was the beginning of the end of slavery.

Luke did whatever he could to educate himself. He would get Luvenia books whenever he could, the master not knowing what he was up to, of course. Sometimes, late at night, when everybody up at the Big House was asleep, that's when they got a chance to study a little bit.

Luke had a place way down in the woods. He thought the place would be hidden. He planted himself some pumpkins and he raised a few hogs and chickens.

Once, his master saw him when he was bringing one of his prized pumpkins to the house. "Where did you get that?" his master said.

"I planted it, I grew it," Luke told him.

"I'm going to take that," his master said.

"This is mine, this is mine," Luke said.

"No, it isn't yours," his master said. "You are my property and property can't own property."

That made Luke so angry, that's when he decided to change his name to Smith. He had been an Oldfield up till then.

When the Civil War came, Luke heard that if you ran away and made it to Fort Totten, in New Bern, you'd be free. So, one night, Luke got the family together and crossed the White Oak River. The two older children, Luvenia and Anthony, were able to walk and swim the river all right. But they just barely made it. The water was up to her nose. Luke had to come back and save her. Luke took the smaller children on his back. You know it was hard on them all, it had to be. They were so frightened. But then they had their freedom when they got to New Bern.

Luvenia became a midwife and a doctor of sorts. Everybody would come to her. I have a scar on my leg. I was about 6, I suppose, when I hurt it. I was sort of tomboyish-like and I was being bad and I was told to quit climbing. I had jumped off a bench which had a nail sticking out of it and it cut me really, just like you would open a fish. The bigger kids grabbed me up and took me to find my grandma. A place like that today would require 20 stitches, I would say. But after she rinsed the cut off, she took an egg, cracked an egg, and—you know that little white skin that's inside the egg shell? She peeled that off, out of the raw egg. She put it right over the wound, and sort of took her hands and brought it together like and put a cloth—didn't have any bandages then— and it knitted back.

Luvenia knew every herb you could mention. Lion's tongue, an herb with striped leaves that grows near the swamp, was good for the kidneys. Rabbit tobacco is good for colds, coughs, bronchitis, asthma. Mullein is good for swelling. Red oak bark was supposed to cleanse the blood. Green pine needles were supposed to open up your breathing passages. Peach tree leaves were good for swelling. Huckleberry leaves was a good cure for diabetes. Pepper grass is better than Tums. It's a weed that grows about this tall, and small leaves, and it tastes better than turnip greens. Real good.

Once, when grandma was still a slave, the mistress's little girl wandered off and fell in a well. Everybody was concerned and upset, and Luvenia went out, found her, and pulled the girl out of the well. She was a little girl herself, about 6 years old. Her mistress was so happy that she said: "I'm going to really reward you." Luvenia came up to the house. She would always have to go around to the back of the house, you know. "Here's you a nice biscuit and a piece of ham," her mistress said. My grandmother said that ham biscuit was just like a thousand dollars to her then!

My grandmother passed away in 1941. Toward the end, she often talked about being lonely. Nobody still around had been through what she had been through. She told these stories again and again. She drilled them into us. She knew that, from time to time, hard times would come upon us, and, sure enough, she was right. She wanted us to know what she had been through. She meant us never to forget.

From David Cecelski,
"Hattie Brown: A Freedom Story,"
Raleigh News & Observer, August 9, 1998.
The interview with Mrs. Brown was conducted by David Cecelski for the Southern Oral History Program at the University of North Carolina at Chapel Hill.

NATURE REMEMBERS

When I was growing up by the Neuse River, we already knew something was not right. Fish had not yet started dying by the millions, and nobody would hear of *Pfiesteria piscicida*, the fish-killing algae, for another twenty-five years. But we knew not to swim in the river. The shad fishery, once the state's largest, had disappeared. And I still remember how, after a sudden thunderstorm capsized our boat off Minnesott Beach, I found my clothes soggy with a dull brown silt that I had never seen in nature.

As I got older, the Neuse screamed that it was dying. Fishkills, algal blooms, and dead zones became annual events. I even found signs posted at Slocum Creek, a Neuse tributary near our home, warning us not to eat the fish because of the danger of nickel, cadmium, and other heavy-metal poisoning.

How did the water quality in the Neuse and our other estuaries get so bad? The cast of long-time culprits is pretty clear: agricultural runoff, land clearing, industrial waste, municipal sewage. But we really did not know their impact on water quality before monitoring began in earnest in the 1970s. A recent phenomenon has also been added to the list of culprits: corporate hog farming.

What was water quality like before urban growth and phosphate mining, before chemical factories and pulp mills? And in the case of the anoxia (oxygen depletion) and eutrophication (nutrient overloading) that precipitate many fishkills, how can we sort out climatic influences from human causes?

Until I met Sherri Cooper, I assumed that these were unanswerable questions. Cooper, a paleoecologist at the Duke University Wetland Center, got interested in the North Carolina coast as a young girl, when she visited her grandmother's home at Core Point on the Pamlico River. Now, she believes that the emerging science of paleoecology can provide at least some of the answers about what we have lost, how we lost it, and what we might regain if our estuaries can be saved.

Paleoecology is the study of living things and their environment in the past. The word sounds arcane, but it really expresses a common-sense idea: *Nature remembers.* Most people are aware of at least a few of the clues used by paleoecologists to decipher ecological history. Tree rings are one. By studying a core sample from a venerable bald cypress growing, say, in the Three Sisters Swamp along the Black River, a paleoecologist can recover a memory of rainfall as far back as when Jesus walked the earth. In the spacing and thickness of the cypress's rings, a trained eye can see hurricanes, droughts, fires, floods, and the rise and fall of rivers.

Paleoecology is much more varied than studying tree rings, but you get the idea: *Nature remem-*

bers. Most of nature's clues to the past are not initially obvious. The history of forests, swamps, and seas is entombed in ecological remnants— pollen grains, chemical traces, river sediments, microscopic fossils. The paleoecologist's job is to scoop up these shards of the past and put them back together.

Until 1979, when Cooper's mentor, Grace Brush at Johns Hopkins University, traced the history of human influence on Chesapeake Bay, few marine scientists believed that paleoecological methods would work in estuaries. They assumed that strong currents and tides scattered sediments, wore away fossils, washed pollen out to sea. In the Chesapeake, Brush showed that she could successfully profile ecological changes dating back far earlier than the first European colonists. Later, Brush and Cooper teamed up to do a path-breaking study of anoxia in Chesapeake Bay, published in the journal *Science* in 1991.

Now Cooper is using a similar approach in North Carolina. With the support of the North Carolina Water Resources Research Institute, she has begun to document the history of water quality in the Neuse and Pamlico estuaries. In the summer of 1997, she collected 2¾- to 5-foot sediment cores from 7 sites. She divided her samples into 2-centimeter sections and dated them using lead-210, cesium-137, and radiocarbon techniques. The

Sherri Cooper in Dr. Ruth Patrick's office, Academy of Natural Sciences of Philadelphia, July 1990

Courtesy of Sherri Cooper

sediments were deposited on the estuary bottom a little bit every year, leaving a stratigraphic record that started with the present at the top layer and went back in time through the deeper sediments. Her deepest samples were laid down about 2,000 years ago.

To analyze the estuarine sediments, Cooper uses her full box of paleoecologist's tools. Her methods are ingenious. One involves collecting pollen fossils preserved in the sediments. Ragweed pollen is an especially interesting gauge of land clearing because this native plant proliferates in disturbed land. Cooper uses a measurement of ragweed pollen as an indicator of land clearing fifty, a hundred, and even a thousand years ago.

She also looks for chemical clues to anoxia and eutrophication. These clues include concentrations of organic carbon, nitrogen, phosphorus, silica, sulfur, and pyritic iron. Each tells her something different about the estuaries in the past. Historic levels of nitrogen and phosphorus are important, for instance, because nutrient enrichment is linked to the depletion of oxygen in estuarine waters. High nutrient levels often cause algal blooms that far exceed the ecosystem's ability to recycle them. When the unconsumed algae eventually die, they sink to the bottom, spurring an increase in the bacteria that help them decay. As the dead algae break down, the bacteria use up the available oxygen, leading to anoxic conditions for other estuarine life.

Though a relatively minor part of Cooper's study, her tests for sulfur levels are another good illustration of the imaginative ways that chemical traces can be used to track ecological changes in the Neuse and Pamlico. Estuarine sediments harbor anaerobic bacteria—that is, bacteria that do not tolerate oxygen. Unlike their oxygen-loving cousins, anaerobic bacteria metabolize naturally occurring sulfur, in the process changing the sulfate form found in seawater to a reduced form known as sulfide. Being highly soluble, sulfate mixes with estuarine waters and washes away. But sulfide is much more likely to combine with metals naturally occurring in estuarine waters and settle into bottom sediments. Thus, when Cooper finds a high level of sulfur in a sediment layer, she knows that the estuary suffered from a lack of oxygen at that time.

I know it is a complicated lesson in geochemistry, but I hope the point is clear: *Nature remembers.* In this case, sulfur levels help to map the levels of oxygen available to estuarine life across the ages.

Cooper's study of fossilized diatoms is another intriguing way to explore the history of water quality. Diatoms are a distinctive kind of microscopic algae and one of the most common

DR. COOPER'S RESEARCH TEAM ON THE NEUSE RIVER ESTUARY
Courtesy of Sherri Cooper

ANALYZING SEDIMENT CORES AT THE DUKE UNIVERSITY WETLAND CENTER
Courtesy of Sherri Cooper

types of phytoplankton in our estuaries. Diatoms and other phytoplankton form the critical first rung in the estuarine food chain. They are the basis of all our commercial and recreational fisheries. Lose the phytoplankton and you lose the fried shrimp and stuffed flounder.

Diatoms are useful in paleoecological research because they have a silica shell, known as a frustule. The frustule has two overlapping parts, like a pillbox and its lid. Because it is almost pure silica, the frustule is preserved in the sediments after the diatom dies. And because each species of diatom has a unique frustule, all the species can be identified under a microscope.

Diatom species are numerous—Cooper counted more than 240 in her sediment cores from the Neuse and Pamlico estuaries. And she expects to find more, based on her research in Chesapeake Bay, where she has counted more than 400. Some thrive in salt water, others in brackish water, others in fresh water. In fact, the species of diatoms in an estuary sample differ depending on a whole range of environmental conditions—not just salinity, but also light, pH, nutrient levels, substrate, temperature, and pollution.

Thus Cooper can identify the diatoms in a sediment sample and tell a great deal about the kind of water conditions in which they lived. It is like seeing an alligator, a cottonmouth snake, and a bald cypress; you do not need to get your feet wet to know you are in a swamp. In this case, the presence or absence of certain species of diatoms helps Cooper recognize the historic levels of eutrophication, salinity, and turbidity.

Cooper has only begun to reconstruct the history of water quality in the Neuse and Pamlico estuaries, but some interesting findings already stand out. Perhaps most importantly, her core samples show relatively few changes in water quality until the twentieth century. (Her preliminary results, however, seem to indicate an intriguing rise in ragweed pollen counts in the fourteenth century. I cannot wait to see how Cooper will explain this. A sudden rise in Algonquian settlement? A massive fire?)

Truly dramatic changes in water quality show up in samples from after World War II. Since 1950, sedimentation rates, nutrient levels, and trace-metal flux have increased significantly, sometimes by an order of magnitude.

Cooper's sediment samples also show a striking decline in the number of diatom species over the last five decades. Diatom diversity has declined by nearly 50 percent in the Pamlico estuary. There have also been telling changes in the kinds of diatoms buried in the estuarine sediments since 1950. These changes chronicle growth in eutrophication, turbidity, sedimentation, freshwater flow, and industrial pollution.

Sunghea Kim, one of Cooper's students,

PARALIA SULCATA, A COMMON DIATOM IN ESTUARINE WATERS
Courtesy of Sherri Cooper

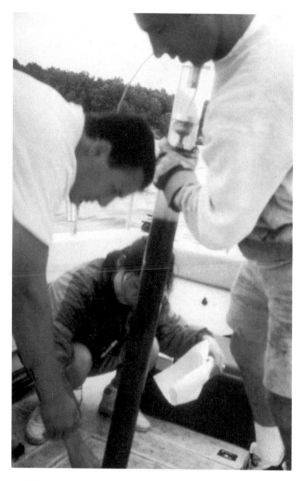

conducted another paleoecological study of estuarine sediments as part of a master's project. The study indicated that trace metals in surface waters of the Neuse and Pamlico estuaries have risen dramatically over the last fifty years. Those trace metals include cadmium, nickel, chromium, and arsenic. Many have reached quantities that exceed the United States Environmental Protection Agency's "threshold effect levels"—that is, the point at which the trace metals affect the estuarine ecology and may start to have an impact on human health.

Cooper hopes to follow other paleoecological clues in the future. Fossilized foraminifera—which resemble microscopic conch shells—are good indicators of salinity levels. Charcoal tells of fire history. Seeds help chronicle changes in submerged aquatic vegetation. Algal pigments preserved in estuarine sediments reveal variations in phytoplankton communities as a whole. All of these natural clues hold tremendous potential for understanding more about the history of water quality in the Neuse and Pamlico estuaries.

Paleoecology also holds a more general lesson. I have long taken for granted that each of us makes a lasting impression on the people whose lives we touch. A simple kindness, a loving gesture, a cruel remark, an unthinking slight—they all leave indelible marks on a human soul. Now, because of Cooper's work, I realize that we also make a lasting impression on every place we touch.

After all, nature remembers.

ALL GOOD THINGS

When I began writing these essays, I never expected to do so much research in a boat. The tools of a historian's trade are usually old books and archives, not coastal swamps and tidal creeks.

But early on, I learned that I had to get out and see a place if I really wanted to understand its past. Even our wildest swamps have a natural history—sometimes gradual, other times cataclysmic—that has been influenced by settlement, exploitation, and other human practices. Most of this past has never been written down and is often not apparent, but you can find traces of it in the land itself if you spend the time and look closely. My canoe and kayak trips have helped me to visualize the coastal landscape at different points in our past and to see ourselves reflected in the ways that we have left our mark on the land.

On many of my forays on coastal waterways, I have been extremely fortunate to have my brother, Richard, as a companion and guide. Richard is the founder and director of Carolina Ocean Studies, an environmental education group that conducts wonderful field trips for schoolchildren. Based at Carolina Beach, Richard is also one of the most expert swamp guides in all of North Carolina. He has an unusually good feel for our coastal swamps, blackwater rivers, and tidewater creeks. It has been a privilege—as well as a lot of fun—to learn from him.

Richard has a keen eye for the human relics

that one finds even in the most remote swamps. A tar pit or rosin mound indicates a site where naval stores were produced, hence where a longleaf pine forest once stood. A tangle of narrow-gauge railroad track reveals that the swamp forest was timbered, most likely between 1880 and 1920, when Northern lumber companies moved into the old-growth forests of the South. Coils of copper wire and rusted barrels are of course evidence of the moonshine liquor industry that thrived on the Carolina coast during Prohibition. The East Lake and "CCC" (Craven County Corn) brands of homemade whiskey were famous in speakeasies from Norfolk to Boston. And when we stumble upon a sunken shad boat on a creek off the Alligator River or a hand-hewn bow net hidden along the White Oak River, we know that we have discovered traces of the springtime fishery that was the largest in the state in the late nineteenth century.

Other times, when we run up against cypress pilings on the waterfronts of tiny river communities like Rockyhock and Colerain, we are reminded of the great herring fisheries that flourished in the Albemarle Sound vicinity before the Civil War. Using seines that were often a mile and a half in length, thousands of slaves and free black fishermen caught the herring as they migrated out of the Atlantic to spawn in tidewater rivers. The pil-

ings mark the old sheds where the laborers headed and salted the herring by the millions.

The canals that pass through coastal swamps also reveal a great deal about the past. Sometimes, all you notice is a narrow, all-too-straight line of visibility through a cypress swamp, but you can bet that it is an old canal once used to float white oak timbers, cypress shingles, and cedar staves to a mill. Along intertidal marshes, I have inadvertently paddled into a labyrinth of intersecting, narrow canals, a sign of rice cultivation in the slavery era, when large gangs of men and women in bondage cultivated the "golden grain" along the Lower Cape Fear. In places like Lake Phelps and Lake Mattamuskeet, I have followed other, larger canals that date to the late eighteenth and early nineteenth centuries, when slaves dug canals to drain swampland for agriculture and to raft crops and lumber to market.

In my travels, I have floated down even larger passages, known as "ships' canals," that bring to life the golden age of canal building between the American Revolution and the Civil War. During that period, many political leaders believed that ships' canals held the greatest promise for overcoming the navigational hazards of North Carolina's shallow sounds and dangerous, shifting inlets. Between 1794 and 1805, for example, slaves dug the twenty-two-mile-long Dismal Swamp

RICHARD CECELSKI STANDS NEXT TO A BALD CYPRESS ON THE BLACK RIVER.
THIS PHOTOGRAPH WAS TAKEN AT EXTREME LOW WATER.

Courtesy of Yvonne Cecelski

Canal to serve as a shipping route between Albemarle Sound and Chesapeake Bay and to skirt the dangerous swash and bar at Ocracoke Inlet.

Though it was antiquated by the opening of the Albemarle and Chesapeake Canal in 1859, the Dismal Swamp Canal had lasting consequences that had nothing to do with shipping. The canal blocked the Great Dismal Swamp's natural water flow from west to east, which eventually dried up the vast wetlands east of the canal and opened them for agriculture. The canal also lowered water levels throughout the moister parts of the Great Dismal, drying out the highly combustible upper layers of peat during summer droughts. Even as early as 1860, unprecedentedly hot peat fires burned much of the old-growth forests of cypress, juniper, and gum in the Great Dismal.

Millponds also have a story to tell. Quite often, Richard and I stumble upon old millponds along remote blackwater creeks. We frequently discover relics of the mills' dams and foundations. When on a millpond, I find it easy to imagine what much of our coastal landscape looked like from the Revolutionary War well into the twentieth century, when millponds could be found in practically every tidewater community. Local people dammed creeks and harnessed the water's flow to power sawmills and gristmills.

I spent one of the best days of my life paddling in Merchants Millpond, formed late in the eighteenth century when a group of Gates County merchants dammed Lassiter Swamp. Today, it is part of a state park that rents canoes and campsites to the public.

More often, though, I go to Morton's Millpond near my family's homeplace. I usually paddle north along the Harlowe and Clubfoot Creek Canal and arrive at the old millpond an hour or two before twilight. An osprey will still be fishing at that hour, and I am likely to see wood ducks, herons, and maybe a gallinule or two before they settle down for the night. The place is bursting with life: dragonflies and lightning bugs, fish hitting the water, and often an otter or muskrat.

Millponds, like all wetlands, are an example of what ecologists refer to as an ecotone, a transitional zone between two diverse ecological communities. Ecotones support life native to each of the two communities (woods and river, for instance), as well as plants and animals endemic to only the ecotone. The heightened diversity and density of life in these transitional zones—a phenomenon known as the "edge effect"—is what makes millponds so remarkably rich in life.

That is also true for beaver ponds. Beavers are a keystone species, whose dams create entire ecosystems that provide habitat and food for a wide range of birds, fish, amphibians, and other animals. Their ponds were once a ubiquitous part of the coastal landscape, filling tens of thousands of acres and providing a remarkable ecotone for all kinds of life. Exterminated two centuries ago by the fur trade and by farmers irate at flooded fields, beavers have only recently started making a comeback in many parts of eastern North Carolina. I never saw them when I was a boy, but I will never forget the first beaver pond I encountered, off Devil's Gut between Williamston and Jamesville. Now, I find that there is nothing nicer than hearing a beaver's tail slap the water when I am spending a night in a swamp.

Sometimes when I am staying overnight in a coastal swamp, I get a glimpse of an even more distant past. It is often not easy to find a dry campsite in a swamp forest. A few times, I have had to paddle well into the night before finding a place to rest my head. More than once on waking the next morning, I have discovered clusters of arrowheads and shards of pottery around my camp, letting me know that I was hardly the first person who found shelter on that knoll or hammock. The coastal Algonquians—or their ancestors—used these same places for fishing camps long before European contact in the sixteenth century. A little hammock along Bennett's Creek in Chowan County is one such place that comes to mind.

For all my historical musings, my special fondness for coastal swamps has little to do with the past. Maybe it is in my blood. Though I did not spend much time as a youngster in the Lakes Pocosin, I grew up on the edge of that swampy wilderness, part of Croatan National Forest east of New Bern. Certainly, my family got bitten by enough mosquitoes that we ought to have some of that pocosin in our blood. Or maybe it is because I have had so many good times poking around these blackwater rivers and swamps with Richard. Then, too, I find a solace and tranquility in them that eludes me amidst the usual chaos of my life.

Above all, I am haunted by the fragility of these freshwater wetlands—our most endangered and underappreciated coastal habitats. Everybody admires the beauty of ocean beaches and salt marshes, and I think most people understand their importance for tourism and the seafood industry. But far fewer people have had the chance to fall in love with the natural beauty and ecological uniqueness of these coastal wetlands—the cypress swamps, blackwater creeks, river bottom lands, pine savannas, pocosins, and Carolina bays.

Once covering more than 3 million acres, these coastal wetlands were reduced to less than half a million acres by 1973. Vast wetlands like the Green Swamp, once one of the largest swamplands in

North America, have vanished. We have lost thousands more acres of wetlands in the last couple of decades, especially since timber companies figured out how to convert pocosins into profitable pine plantations by using new drainage techniques and relying on the heavy aerial spraying of fertilizers and pesticides. Some of the nation's greatest pocosins, such as the East Dismal Swamp in Washington and Beaufort Counties, have nearly disappeared in this way. If these unsung wildernesses are going to be saved, it will have to happen soon.

Though I often find reasons for despair at the coast's future, I also find much cause for hope. One of the greatest pleasures of exploring my native land for these essays was that I came to know so many people—natives and newcomers alike—who are determined to protect our coastal wetlands and who yearn to know more about their history. Again and again, they renewed my spirits and inspired in me a fierce hope for the future.

I also could not be more grateful for their hospitality. As I traveled the coast, untold numbers of local people gave me directions to hard-to-find spots. They fed me suppers of fish stew and oyster fritters. They gave me shelter when I was caught in storms. Above all, I appreciate those elderly men and women who quietly took me aside and shared an ancestor's diary or the location of old ruins that revealed forgotten parts of our coastal past.

I do not know what I did, if anything, to deserve their neighborliness and their stories, but I will never cease to cherish them. And if you are one of those people I have not yet happened upon, I hope we will meet before long. I am the one in the small boat paddling into the swamp and, as always, into the past.

ACKNOWLEDGMENTS

I am grateful to Kathy Hart, Carla Burgess, Jeannie Faris Norris, Daun Daemon, Debbi Sykes Braswell, Katie Mosher, and all the editors at *Coastwatch* magazine for their careful editing of my original essays. I would also like to thank the archivists, curators, and librarians who were such an indispensable help to my research: Beverly Tetterton at the New Hanover County Public Library; George Stevenson at the North Carolina State Archives; Brian Edwards at the Outer Banks History Center; Alice Cotten, Bob Anthony, and Jerry Cotten at the North Carolina Collection of the University of North Carolina at Chapel Hill; Victor Jones at the New Bern/Craven County Public Library; Karen Amspacher at the Core Sound Waterfowl Museum; Al Potts and Lisa Whitman-Grice at the Onslow County Histori-cal Museum; Harry Warren at the Cape Fear Museum; Scott Taylor at the Duke University Marine Laboratory; and Connie Mason at the North Carolina Maritime Museum. I owe extra thanks to Wynne Dough of the Outer Banks History Center and Wilson Angley of the Research Office at the North Carolina Division of Archives and History, both of whom scoured early drafts of many of the essays for factual errors. I would also like to recognize Norma Llongo, one of my students when I taught at Duke University in 1996. Norma's path-breaking research on Allen Parker's *Recollections of Slavery Times* was a tremendous help to my essay on Parker. Jeff Crow opened a hundred doors for me. Carolyn Sakowski and the staff at John F. Blair have been gems to work with. And I would never have gotten the final draft of the book ready without my research and editorial assistant, Alison Waldenberg, for whom all things are indeed possible.

I would also like to thank the friends and family members who have been my traveling companions on these explorations of the tidewater past. My brother, Richard, is a font of local wisdom gleaned from being a great waterman and hanging out with some of the finest old-time swampers. I could not have written this book without him. I have also relied heavily on the knowledge of his wife, Sandie, who teaches marine biology at New Hanover High School in Wilmington. Jake, Lauren, Amber-Dog, Liz, Michael, Nicky, Jonathan, Elaine, and Jesus have been, along with my children, Vera and Guy, the best rambling buddies in the world. Perri, Hope, Sam, and the men, women, and children of the Women's Dinner Group have also been true-blue friends, and I hope we will soon be on the road again. And I would go into any swamp, anytime, with Bland Simpson, whose faith in this book meant nearly as much to me as our trips into the Dark Woods. Kat Charron is a tremendous help in everything I write, and I promise I will get her that fried mullet I owe her. Glenda Gilmore gave me the idea of turning these essays into a book; she may have recognized what I was trying to do with them, at the deepest level, before I did. And Paige Raibmon, as fine an outdoorswoman as there is, generously shared with me both her unsurpassed knowledge of environmental history and her passion for loons and other waterfowl.

My wife, Laura, was by far the greatest treasure that I brought back from my morning trips to Shackleford Banks all those winters ago. On our first, rather accidental date, she accompanied me out to Shackleford when she was on a weekend visit to the marine laboratory in Beaufort—which no doubt has more to do with my fond memories of those mornings than conch chowder and roasted oysters. Laura has remained a steadfast friend, editor, and swamping companion ever since. Somehow, despite her own demanding work, she finds time to read and reread and reread again my writing. And when I burn out, she is always there to rescue me. I am eternally grateful to her.

I could never express my debt to Tim Tyson. As good a historian as there is, he has generously shared his editorial genius and has been a boon companion on adventures far and wide. No matter how rough the waters, I can always count on Tim to get that determined (many might say foolhardy) gleam in his eye and head us directly into the gale. Only God knows how we have survived this long. But make no mistake: not even in the worst storm have I once longed to return to the safety of the shore.

INDEX